50 Android Hacks

50 Android Hacks

CARLOS SESSA

MANNING

SHELTER ISLAND

Manning Publications Co.
20 Baldwin Road
PO Box 261
Shelter Island, NY 11964

Development editor: Cynthia Kane
Technical proofreader: Cyril Mottier
Copyeditor: Benjamin Berg
Proofreader: Katie Tennant
Typesetter: Dottie Marsico
Cover designer: Marija Tudor

ISBN 9781617290565
Printed in the United States of America
1 2 3 4 5 6 7 8 9 10 – MAL – 18 17 16 15 14 13

Al milagro que hizo esto posible

(To the miracle that made this possible)

brief contents

contents

6 *Working with lists and adapters 77*

foreword

Android as an ecosystem is expanding rapidly in all directions. Every day manufacturers introduce new devices and form factors, consumers purchase and activate over one million devices, and users download and try new apps. It's the job of developers (yourself included, hopefully) to fill this ecosystem with beautiful, engaging, and deeply fulfilling applications through which users can better interpret and interact with their world.

As a platform, Android was birthed in late 2003 by former employees of Danger (the company behind the popular Sidekick phones). In 2005 the company driving Android was acquired by Google, and three years later the HTC Dream (G1) was released as the first consumer device running Android. Over the next three years the hardware and platform were heavily iterated, but Android remained solely a phone operating system.

In 2011 Google introduced two new form factors for the Android: tablets and TV. This represented the first official deviation from phones as the device of choice and sparked manufacturer interest in other devices. Android now runs on laptops, wristwatches, video game consoles, and car stereos. It can only be expected that in the future the number of devices supporting Android will continue to grow.

As application developers, it's extremely important that you understand the diversity of the platform and the direction in which it's heading. Creating content on Android is no longer as simple as designing for a phone-sized screen held in portrait orientation. While this does mean more work for the developer creating apps, the end result is a vastly more pleasant experience for the user, regardless of which device your content is consumed on.

In developing applications there are three major things that you'll need aside from your own creativity and desire to develop: the platform documentation, the open source community, and glue to hold everything together. The platform documentation is easy, since the latest version is always hosted at http://developer.android.com. The open source community is spread across GitHub, Google Code, Stack Overflow, and the like, providing libraries, code snippets, and design patterns for simplifying development. You still need something to tie these disjointed pieces together as one cohesive app. If it were as simple as arranging a few building blocks, everyone would be developing applications. This book is that glue.

Contained in the book are examples of how to solve common problems that arise in Android development. Some are relatively trivial and some quite complex. What they share, however, is being loosely or sparsely documented facets of app development which often cause developers pain. *50 Android Hacks* is not meant as a sole resource for learning or mastering Android development, but rather exists to fill in the cracks.

It's a great task to craft an app that's dynamic enough to support Android's growing device diversity. With the knowledge provided by this book, accompanied by that of similar print and online sources, it's my hope that you're more empowered to develop and publish apps. Beyond this, while I am a developer just like you, I am also an avid Android user and patiently await that next great application. Perhaps you will be the one to write it.

JAKE WHARTON
ANDROID ENGINEER

preface

I started learning about Android back in 2009. Android version 1.5 had just been released, and it showed a lot of potential.

In July 2009, thanks to a friend living in Australia, I got my first Android-powered device, an HTC Magic with Android version 1.5. To be honest, it processed more slowly than I expected, but I started testing the APIs and creating apps that I wanted to have on my cell phone. I sensed that Android would get a lot of attention and I knew that if I managed to create an application, it would be available to a lot of people.

I was proved right—not long afterward, there was a kick-off for Android development, which soon grew bigger and bigger. Suddenly a lot of tools and third-party libraries supporting the Android platform emerged—everything from game frameworks, like cocos2d-x, to build systems, like Apache Maven.

In November 2010 I was asked to review a book from Manning Publications called *Android in Practice* (www.manning.com/collins/). Delving deep into Manning's work, it occurred to me that I could write a book about Android development using a different approach. I wanted to imitate Joshua Bloch's *Effective Java* (www.amazon.com/ Effective-Java-2nd-Joshua-Bloch/dp/0321356683), providing tips and patterns I had learned over all my years of developing for the Android platform.

Essentially, I wanted to gather together in one book every Android tip I have learned and provide some degree of documentation for it. That's what *50 Android Hacks* is all about: a collection of tips gathered in the process of developing different Android applications.

Something I enjoyed about *Effective Java* was that the book doesn't have any particular order and I could read various sections, learning something different from each of them. After some time, I would go back to the book and find a different application for the project I was working on. I kept that in mind while writing this book. I imagine the reader investigating a hack while going to work or before going to sleep, getting new ideas for the project they're working on.

I'm already using this book on my new projects, copying the sample code for certain tasks and using its examples to explain to my coworkers certain patterns. It's proven to be useful for myself, and I hope it will be useful for you as well.

While writing the book and samples, I set the minimum SDK to 1.6. Most of the hacks in the book work in Android version 1.6 onward unless mentioned. You'll notice that there are hacks specific to the newest Android versions, but most of them are recommendations or ideas that would work for every version. Every hack has an icon identifying the minimum SDK it will work with.

So pick a hack of interest to you from the table of contents and start reading. I hope you learn as much reading this book as I learned writing it.

acknowledgments

When reading acknowledgments in other books, I'm always surprised by the number of people the author thanks. I now understand how big the list can be, and as I write these words I'm nervous that I may be forgetting someone.

First of all, I want to thank Cynthia Kane, my development editor. She helped me manage the book. She pointed out every single thing that needed a change, dealt with my inadequacies in English, and helped me understand the key parts of creating a book. Almost every single line I wrote needed a fix, and while it was sometimes frustrating for Cynthia, the result of these repeated iterations is a book of which I am proud.

Another key player was Nicholas Chase. Nick is in charge of support for the Manning XML schema and the authoring tool. Fortunately, Nick was online on Skype every time I had an question for him.

The rest of the Manning team also played a big part. Some of the people who worked with me are Ozren Harlovic, Kevin Sullivan, Tara McGoldrick Walsh, Benjamin Berg, Katie Tennant, Candace Gillhoolley, Martin Murtonen, Michael Stephens, and Maureen Spencer.

Thanks to the collaborators: William Sanville (Hack 40: Last-in-first-out image loading; and Hack 41: Building databases with ORMLite); Chris King (Hack 26: Adding section headers to a ListView); and Christopher Orr (Hack 50: Using Jenkins to deal with device diversity). They lent their expertise to complete these areas.

Thanks to Cyril Mottier, who took an in-depth look at the book and didn't hesitate to tell me which parts he hated and wanted to change. He kept the bar very high and I enjoyed working with him. Merci beaucoup!

Thanks to my partners at NASA Trained Monkeys, who helped me out by reading a lot and making recommendations. Most of the cool hack titles came from their wild imaginations.

Thanks to the Android community itself, and a special thanks to the people who contribute to open source libraries (just to mention a few names: Michael Burton, Manfred Moser, Matthias Käppler, Jake Wharton, Jeremy Feinstein, the cocos2d-x team, Jan Berkel, Jeff Gilgelt, Xavi Rigau, Chris Banes, James Brechtel, and Dmitry Skiba).

Thanks to everyone who reviewed the book. The reviews helped me identify what was missing and what topics needed more attention. Getting positive reviews from people I admire was very rewarding. Thanks to the following reviewers for finding the time to read the book; I hope you learned something from it: Adam Koch, Alberto Pose, Bill Cruise, Christian Badenas, Frank Ableson, Ignacio Luciani, Jeff Goldschrafe, Joshua Skinner, Matthias Käppler, Maximiliano Gomez Vidal, "Ming," Octavian Damiean, Paul Butcher, Robi Sen, Roger Binns, Shan Coster, Suzanne Alexandra, and Will Turnage.

Thanks to my family and friends—you did a great job supporting me!

And last but not least, thank you, Mili, for being there every time I needed you. I love you.

about this book

Android is a project with a lot of momentum. The first Android release happened on September 23, 2008, and by the end of 2010 it had become the leading smartphone platform.

Every time there's a new release, a new set of APIs and possibilities show up. While Android version 1.5 (Donut) only worked in the HTC Dream, right now Android runs in many devices from cellphone to TVs, and on different sizes of tablets and laptops.

This causes two big problems when developing for Android. First, you have to deal with different types of supported devices. While there are lots of ways of dealing with different screen sizes and screen density, you need to create an app that works, and looks great, in every device. Also, targeting every possible Android-powered device might result in different user experiences. The user won't interact in the same way with a cellphone as with a TV.

The second problem is how long the Android versions stay alive. The story is always the same: with a new Android version, we get new APIs. A new API would be an excellent addition to your app, but as a developer you still need to support older versions, because not everyone will get the update and also because it may take a lot of time to reach your main target audience.

You'll need to choose if you want to add the new API functionality and release an app just for people using the newest Android version, or go with a hybrid approach where some functionalities are only available in newer versions.

I've created this book to help you out, because when you're developing for Android, all the decisions are in your hands. *50 Android Hacks* offers a problem/solution approach to tasks you might encounter while developing, but also ways to enhance what's already there.

What is Android?

Android is an open source operating system based on Linux. In the beginning, it was just for cell phones, but now it works on tablets, TVs, computers, and even car stereos. It has been gaining a lot of momentum in the mobile scene and is now used in more than 50% of mobile devices.

The apps that run on an Android-powered device are usually coded in Java and it has a powerful SDK that allows the developer to create different types of applications. Android allows developers to customize almost everything. For example, you can create custom wallpapers, custom keyboards, and custom home screens, things you wouldn't imagine doing in other platforms.

Who should read this book?

This book is intended for people who are already developing with Android. I assume you know how to program in Java and the basic concepts of the Android platform.

There are hacks intended for people taking their first steps with the Android platform, and there are hacks for advanced developers. If you're developing an Android app, skim through the book; I'm sure you'll find something that will help you.

To find out if this book is for you, consider these questions:

- Are you developing for Android?
- Have you found yourself scratching your head, trying to think of better solutions to your problems?
- Are you looking for new ways of addressing your programming issues?
- Do you want to find out how other people are handling similar problems?

How to use this book

My recommendation is that, before you read about a hack, you first compile and run the sample code. That will give you a better understanding of what we'll do in each example. Apart from that, the book doesn't need to be read in any particular order. Feel free to start reading any section that interests you.

Roadmap

While the book is flexible enough to let you go forward and backward between hacks without an issue, you can also read it sequentially.

- Chapter 1, "Working your way around layouts," has four hacks that offer you different layout tips.
- The four hacks in chapter 2, "Creating cool animations," describe different tips for dealing with animations.
- Chapter 3, "View tips and tricks," has nine hacks covering every tip related to views.
- The two hacks in chapter 4, "Tools," give you an overview of available tools apart from the IDE.

- Chapter 5, "Patterns," offers pattern examples in its four hacks that are applicable for Android.
- Chapter 6, "Working with lists and adapters," groups tips about the `ListView` and `Adapter` classes in its seven hacks.
- Two hacks in chapter 7, "Useful libraries," explain how to use third-party libraries in your apps.
- Chapter 8, "Interacting with other languages," shows some examples of coding for Android in programming languages other than Java in one hack focused on Objective-C and one hack discussing Scala.
- Chapter 9, "Ready-to-use snippets," offers six hacks that provide copy-and-paste code snippets.
- The three hacks in chapter 10, "Beyond database basics," state some advanced tips about database usage.
- Chapter 11, "Avoiding fragmentation," includes four hacks that show how to make your app work in different Android versions.
- The final three hacks presented in chapter 12, "Building tools," include tips on how to build your app.

Code conventions and downloads

All the code in the examples used in this book is presented in a `monospace font like this`. Annotations accompany many of the code listings and numbered cueballs are used if longer explanations are needed.

The source code for all of the examples in the book is available for download from the publisher's website at www.manning.com/50AndroidHacks. You can also download the source code from the Google code project. How to get the latest code is explained in the appendix. The sample code is hosted at GitHub. You can download the code here: https://github.com/Macarse/50AH-code.

To run the book samples, you'll need to install

- Eclipse
- Android SDK
- Eclipse Android plugin

If you don't know where to start, I recommend visiting http://developer .android.com/sdk/installing/index.html, where there's an easy step-by-step guide to configuration.

Author Online

The purchase of *50 Android Hacks* includes free access to a private web forum run by Manning Publications, where you can make comments about the book, ask technical questions, and receive help from the author and from other users. To access the forum and subscribe to it, point your web browser to www.manning.com/50AnroidHacks.

This page provides information on how to get on the forum once you are registered, what kind of help is available, and the rules of conduct on the forum.

Manning's commitment to our readers is to provide a venue where a meaningful dialogue between individual readers and between readers and the author can take place. It is not a commitment to any specific amount of participation on the part of the author, whose contribution to the forum remains voluntary (and unpaid). We suggest you try asking the author some challenging questions lest his interest stray!

The Author Online forum and the archives of previous discussions will be accessible from the publisher's website as long as the book is in print.

About the author

Carlos Sessa is a passionate full-time Android developer. He is the cofounder of a mobile development company based in Buenos Aires, Argentina, called NASA Trained Monkeys. His company focuses on mobile development for both Android and iOS platforms.

about the cover illustration

The figure on the cover of *50 Android Hacks* is captioned "A Woodsman." The illustration is taken from a nineteenth-century edition of Sylvain Maréchal's four-volume compendium of regional dress customs published in France. Each illustration is finely drawn and colored by hand. The rich variety of Maréchal's collection reminds us vividly of how culturally apart the world's towns and regions were just 200 years ago. Isolated from each other, people spoke different dialects and languages. On the streets or in the countryside, it was easy to identify where they lived and what their trade or station in life was just by their dress.

Dress codes have changed since then and the diversity by region, so rich at the time, has faded away. It is now hard to tell apart the inhabitants of different continents, let alone different towns or regions. Perhaps we have traded cultural diversity for a more varied personal life—certainly for a more varied and fast-paced technological life.

At a time when it is hard to tell one computer book from another, Manning celebrates the inventiveness and initiative of the computer business with book covers based on the rich diversity of regional life of two centuries ago, brought back to life by Maréchal's pictures.

Working your way around layouts

1

In this chapter, we'll cover tips and recommendations for Android layouts. You'll learn how to create certain types of layouts from scratch as well as how to improve upon existing ones.

Hack 1 Centering views using weights
Android v1.6+

At an Android talk I gave to a group of developers, when I was explaining how to create a view using an XML file, someone asked, "What should I write if I want a button to be centered and 50% of its parent width?" At first I didn't understand what he was asking, but after he drew it on the board, I understood. His idea is shown in figures 1.1 and 1.2.

It looks simple, right? Now take five minutes to try to achieve it. In this hack, we'll look at how to solve this problem using the LinearLayout's android:weightSum attribute in conjunction with the LinearLayout's child android:layout_weight attribute. This might sound like a simple task, but it's something I always ask about in interviews with developers because a lot of them don't know the best way to do this.

Figure 1.1   Button with 50% of its parent width (portrait)

Figure 1.2   Button with 50% of its parent width (landscape)

1.1   Combining weightSum and layout_weight

Android devices have different sizes, and as developers we need to create XML in a way that works for different screen sizes. Hard-coding sizes isn't an option, so we'll need something else to organize our views.

We'll use the `layout_weight` and `weightSum` attributes to fill up any remaining space inside our layout. The documentation for `android:weightSum` (see section 1.3) describes a scenario similar to what we're trying to achieve:

> Defines the maximum weight sum. If unspecified, the sum is computed by adding the `layout_weight` of all of the children. This can be used for instance to give a single child 50% of the total available space by giving it a `layout_weight` of 0.5 and setting the `weightSum` to 1.0.

Imagine we need to place stuff inside a box. The percentage of available space would be the `weightSum` and the `layout_weight` would be the percentage available for each item inside the box. For example, let's say the box has a `weightSum` of 1 and we have two items, *A* and *B*. *A* has a `layout_weight` of 0.25 and *B* has a `layout_weight` of 0.75. So item *A* will have 25% of the box space, while *B* will get the remaining 75%.

The solution to the situation we covered at the beginning of this chapter is similar. We give the parent a certain `weightSum` and give the button half of that value as `android:layout_weight`. The resulting XML follows:

```
<?xml version="1.0" encoding="utf-8"?>
<LinearLayout xmlns:android="http://schemas.android.com/apk/res/android"
```

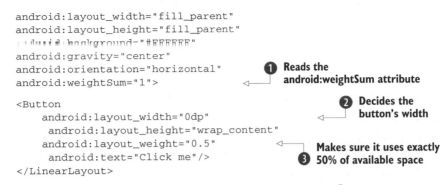

```
android:layout_width="fill_parent"
android:layout_height="fill_parent"
android:background="#FFFFFF"
android:gravity="center"
android:orientation="horizontal"          ❶ Reads the
android:weightSum="1">                        android:weightSum attribute

    <Button                                        ❷ Decides the
        android:layout_width="0dp"                    button's width
         android:layout_height="wrap_content"
        android:layout_weight="0.5"            Makes sure it uses exactly
         android:text="Click me"/>             ❸ 50% of available space
    </LinearLayout>
```

The LinearLayout reads the android:weightSum attribute ❶ and learns that the sum of the weights of its children needs to be 1. Its first and only child is the Button and because the button has its android:layout_width set to 0dp ❷, the LinearLayout knows that it must decide the button's width by the available space given by the android:weightSum. Because the Button has the android:layout_weight set to 0.5 ❸, it will use exactly 50% of the available space.

A possible example would be a 200dp wide LinearLayout with its android:weightSum set to 1. The width of the Button would be calculated as follows:

```
Button's width + Button's weight * 200 / sum(weight)
```

Because the Button's width is 0dp, the Button's weight is 0.5. With the sum(weight) set to 1, the result would be the following:

```
0 + 0.5 * 200 / 1 = 100
```

1.2 The bottom line

Using LinearLayout's weight is important when you want to distribute the available space based on a percentage rather than using hard-coded sizes. If you're targeting Honeycomb and using Fragments, you'll notice that most of the examples place the different Fragments in a layout using weights. Understanding how to use weights will add an important tool to your toolbox.

1.3 External links

http://developer.android.com/reference/android/widget/LinearLayout.html

Hack 2   *Using lazy loading and avoiding replication*
Android v1.6+

When you're creating complex layouts, you may find yourself adding a lot of View-Groups and Views. But making your view hierarchy tree taller will also make it slower.

Creating optimized layouts is fundamental to building an application that runs fast and is responsive to the user.

In this hack, you'll learn how to use the <include /> tag in your XML to avoid replication, and how to use the ViewStub class to lazy load views.

2.1 *Avoid replication using the <include /> tag*

Let's imagine we want to add a footer to every view in our application—something simple, such as a TextView with our application's name. If we have more than one Activity, we might have more than one XML file. Would we copy this TextView to every XML file? What happens if we need to edit it in the future? Copying and pasting would solve the problem, but it doesn't sound efficient. The easiest way to add a footer to our application is to use the <include /> tag. Let's look at how it can help us out.

We use the <include /> tag in XML to add another layout from another XML file. In our example, we'll create our complete view, and at the bottom we'll add the <include /> tag pointing to our footer's layout. One of our Activity's XML files would look like the following:

```xml
<RelativeLayout
  xmlns:android="http://schemas.android.com/apk/res/android"
  android:layout_width="fill_parent"
  android:layout_height="fill_parent">

  <TextView
    android:layout_width="fill_parent"
    android:layout_height="wrap_content"
    android:layout_centerInParent="true"
    android:gravity="center_horizontal"
    android:text="@string/hello"/>

  <include layout="@layout/footer_with_layout_properties"/>

</RelativeLayout/>
```

And the footer_with_layout_properties would look like the following:

```xml
<TextView xmlns:android="http://schemas.android.com/apk/res/android"
  android:layout_width="fill_parent"
  android:layout_height="wrap_content"
  android:layout_alignParentBottom="true"
  android:layout_marginBottom="30dp"
  android:gravity="center_horizontal"
  android:text="@string/footer_text"/>
```

In this first example, we've used the <include /> tag with the only required layout. You might be thinking, "OK, this works because we're using a RelativeLayout for our main XML. What'll happen if one of the XML files is a LinearLayout? android:layout_alignParentBottom="true" wouldn't work because it's a RelativeLayout attribute." That's true. Let's look at the second way to use includes, where we'll place android:layout_* attributes in the <include /> itself.

The following modified main.xml uses the <include /> tag with android:layout_* attributes:

```
<RelativeLayout
  xmlns:android="http://schemas.android.com/apk/res/android"
  android:layout_width="fill_parent"
  android:layout_height="fill_parent">

  <TextView
    android:layout_width="fill_parent"
    android:layout_height="wrap_content"
    android:layout_centerInParent="true"
    android:gravity="center_horizontal"
    android:text="@string/hello"/>

  <include
    layout="@layout/footer"
    android:layout_width="fill_parent"
    android:layout_height="wrap_content"
    android:layout_alignParentBottom="true"
    android:layout_marginBottom="30dp"/>

</RelativeLayout>
```

The following shows the modified footer.xml:

```
<TextView xmlns:android="http://schemas.android.com/apk/res/android"
  android:layout_width="0dp"
  android:layout_height="0dp"
  android:gravity="center"
  android:text="@string/footer_text"/>
```

In this second example, we've let the container of the included footer decide where to place it. Android's issue tracker has reported an issue, which says that the <include /> tag is broken (overriding layout params never works). This is partially true. The problem is that the <include /> tag must specify both android:layout_width and android:layout_height if we want to override any android:layout_* attributes.

Note a small detail about what we've done in this hack. As you can see in the second example, we moved every android:layout_* attribute to the <include /> tag. Take a look at the width and height we placed in the footer.xml file: they're both 0dp. We did this to make users specify a width and height when used together with the <include /> tag. If users don't add them, they won't see the footer because the width and height are zero.

2.2 *Lazy loading views with the ViewStub class*

When designing your layouts, you may have thought about showing a view depending on the context or the user interactions. If you've ever found yourself making a view invisible and then making it visible afterward, you should keep on reading—you'll want to use the ViewStub class.

As an introduction to the ViewStub class, let's take a look at the Android documentation (see section 2.4):

A `ViewStub` is an invisible, zero-sized `View` that can be used to lazily inflate layout resources at runtime. When a `ViewStub` is made visible, or when `inflate()` is invoked, the layout resource is inflated. The `ViewStub` then replaces itself in its parent with the inflated `View` or `Views`.

You already know what a `ViewStub` is, so let's see what you can do with it. In the following example you'll use a `ViewStub` to lazy load a `MapView`. Imagine creating a view with the details about a place. Let's look at two possible scenarios:

- Some venues don't have GPS information
- The user might not need the map

If the venue doesn't have GPS information, you can't place a marker on the map, and if the user doesn't need the map, why load it? Let's place the `MapView` inside a `View-Stub` and let the user decide whether to load the map.

To achieve this, you'll use the following layout:

```xml
<?xml version="1.0" encoding="utf-8"?>
<RelativeLayout
    xmlns:android="http://schemas.android.com/apk/res/android"
    android:layout_width="fill_parent"
    android:layout_height="fill_parent">

  <Button
    android:layout_width="fill_parent"
    android:layout_height="wrap_content"
    android:text="@string/show_map"
    android:onClick="onShowMap"/>

  <ViewStub
        android:id="@+id/map_stub"
        android:layout_width="fill_parent"
        android:layout_height="fill_parent"
    android:layout="@layout/map"
    android:inflatedId="@+id/map_view"/>
</RelativeLayout>
```

It might be obvious, but we'll use the `map_stub` ID to get the `ViewStub` from the `Activity`, and the `layout` attribute tells the `ViewStub` which layout should inflate. For this example, we'll use the following layout for the map:

```xml
<?xml version="1.0" encoding="utf-8"?>
<com.google.android.maps.MapView
  xmlns:android="http://schemas.android.com/apk/res/android"
  android:layout_width="fill_parent"
  android:layout_height="fill_parent"
  android:clickable="true"
  android:apiKey="my_api_key"/>
```

The last attribute we need to discuss is `inflatedId`. The `inflatedId` is the ID that the inflated view will have after we call `inflate()` or `setVisibility()` in the `ViewStub` class. In this example, we'll use `setVisibility(View.VISIBLE)` because we won't do anything else with the `MapView`. If we want to get a reference to the view inflated, the `inflate()` method returns the view to avoid a second call to `findViewById()`.

The code for the `Activity` is simple:

```
public class MainActivity extends MapActivity {

  private View mViewStub;

  @Override
  public void onCreate(Bundle savedInstanceState) {
    super.onCreate(savedInstanceState);
    setContentView(R.layout.main);
    mViewStub = findViewById(R.id.map_stub);
  }

  public void onShowMap(View v) {
    mViewStub.setVisibility(View.VISIBLE);
  }

  ...

}
```

As you can see, we only need to change the `ViewStub` visibility when we want to show the map.

2.3   *The bottom line*

The `<include />` tag is a useful tool to order your layout. If you already created something with the `Fragment` class, you'll notice that using includes is almost the same thing. As you need to do with fragments, your complete view can be a set of includes.

The `<include />` tag offers a nice way to organize the content of your XML files. If you're making a complex layout and the XML gets too big, try creating different parts using includes. The XML becomes easier to read and more organized.

`ViewStub` is an excellent class to lazy load your views. Whenever you're hiding a view and making it visible, depending on the context, try using a `ViewStub`. Perhaps you won't notice the performance boost with only one view, but you will if the view has a large view hierarchy.

2.4   *External links*

http://code.google.com/p/android/issues/detail?id=2863

http://android-developers.blogspot.com.ar/2009/03/
    android-layout-tricks-3-optimize-with.html

http://developer.android.com/reference/android/view/ViewStub.html

Hack 3   *Creating a custom ViewGroup*
Android v1.6+

When you're designing your application, you might have complex views that will show up in different activities. Imagine that you're creating a card game and you want to show the user's hand in a layout similar to figure 3.1. How would you create a layout like that?

Figure 3.1   User's hand in a card game

You might say that playing with margins will be enough for that type of layout. That's true. You can do something similar to the previous figure with a RelativeLayout and add margins to its children. The XML looks like the following:

```xml
<?xml version="1.0" encoding="utf-8"?>
<RelativeLayout
    xmlns:android="http://schemas.android.com/apk/res/android"
    android:layout_width="fill_parent"
    android:layout_height="fill_parent" >

    <View
        android:layout_width="100dp"
        android:layout_height="150dp"
        android:background="#FF0000" />

    <View
        android:layout_width="100dp"
        android:layout_height="150dp"
        android:layout_marginLeft="30dp"
        android:layout_marginTop="20dp"
        android:background="#00FF00" />

    <View
        android:layout_width="100dp"
        android:layout_height="150dp"
        android:layout_marginLeft="60dp"
        android:layout_marginTop="40dp"
        android:background="#0000FF" />

</RelativeLayout>
</FrameLayout>
```

The result of the previous XML can be seen in figure 3.2.

In this hack, we'll look at another way of creating the same type of layout—we'll create a custom View-Group. The benefits of using a custom ViewGroup instead of adding margins by hand in an XML file are these:

- It's easier to maintain if you're using it in different activities.

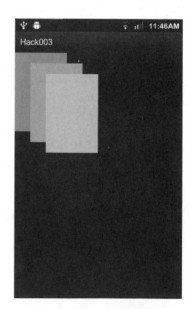

Figure 3.2   Card layout created using the default Android widgets

- You can use custom attributes to customize the position of the `ViewGroup` children.
- The XML will be easier to understand because it'll be more concise.
- If you need to change the margins, you won't need to recalculate by hand every child's margin.

Let's take a look at how Android draws views.

3.1 Understanding how Android draws views

To create a custom `ViewGroup`, you'll need to understand how Android draws views. I won't go into the details, but you'll need to understand the following paragraph from the documentation (see section 3.5), because it explains how you can draw a layout:

> Drawing the layout is a two-pass process: a measure pass and a layout pass. The measuring pass is implemented in `measure(int, int)` and is a top-down traversal of the `View` tree. Each `View` pushes dimension specifications down the tree during the recursion. At the end of the measure pass, every `View` has stored its measurements. The second pass happens in `layout(int, int, int, int)` and is also top-down. During this pass each parent is responsible for positioning all of its children using the sizes computed in the measure pass.

To understand the concept, let's analyze the way to draw a `ViewGroup`. The first step is to measure its width and height, and we do this in the `onMeasure()` method. Inside that method, the `ViewGroup` will calculate its size by going through its children. We'll make the final pass in the `onLayout()` method. Inside this second method, the `View-Group` will lay out its children using the information gathered in the `onMeasure()` pass.

3.2 Creating the CascadeLayout

In this section, we'll code the custom `ViewGroup`. We'll achieve the same result as figure 3.2. Call the custom `ViewGroup`: `CascadeLayout`. The XML using the `Cascade-Layout` follows:

```xml
<?xml version="1.0" encoding="utf-8"?>
<FrameLayout
    xmlns:android="http://schemas.android.com/apk/res/android"
    xmlns:cascade=
    "http://schemas.android.com/apk/res/com.manning.androidhacks.hack003"
    android:layout_width="fill_parent"
    android:layout_height="fill_parent" >

    <com.manning.androidhacks.hack003.view.CascadeLayout
        android:layout_width="fill_parent"
        android:layout_height="fill_parent"

        cascade:horizontal_spacing="30dp"
        cascade:vertical_spacing="20dp" >

        <View
            android:layout_width="100dp"
```

Custom namespace to use custom attributes in the XML

With cascade namespace you can use custom attributes

CascadeLayout used from the XML using its fully qualified name

```
            android:layout_height="150dp"
            android:background="#FF0000" />

        <View
            android:layout_width="100dp"
            android:layout_height="150dp"
            android:background="#00FF00" />

        <View
            android:layout_width="100dp"
            android:layout_height="150dp"
            android:background="#0000FF" />
    </com.manning.androidhacks.hack003.view.CascadeLayout>

</FrameLayout>
```

Now that you know what you need to build, let's get started. The first thing we'll do is define those custom attributes. To do this, we need to create a file called attrs.xml inside the res/values folder, with the following code:

```
<?xml version="1.0" encoding="utf-8"?>
<resources>
    <declare-styleable name="CascadeLayout">
        <attr name="horizontal_spacing" format="dimension" />
        <attr name="vertical_spacing" format="dimension" />
    </declare-styleable>
</resources>
```

We'll also use default values for the horizontal and vertical spacing for those times when the user doesn't specify them. We'll place the default values inside a dimens.xml file inside the res/values folder. The contents of the dimens.xml file are as follows:

```
<?xml version="1.0" encoding="utf-8"?>
<resources>
    <dimen name="cascade_horizontal_spacing">10dp</dimen>
    <dimen name="cascade_vertical_spacing">10dp</dimen>
</resources>
```

After understanding how Android draws views, you might imagine that you need to write a class called CascadeLayout that extends ViewGroup and overrides the onMeasure() and onLayout() methods. Because the code's a bit long, let's analyze it in three separate parts: the constructor, the onMeasure() method, and the onLayout() method. The following code is for the constructor:

```
public class CascadeLayout extends ViewGroup {

  private int mHorizontalSpacing;
  private int mVerticalSpacing;

  public CascadeLayout(Context context, AttributeSet attrs) {
      super(context, attrs);

    TypedArray a = context.obtainStyledAttributes(attrs,
        R.styleable.CascadeLayout);
    try {
      mHorizontalSpacing = a.getDimensionPixelSize(
```

Constructor called when view instance is created from an XML file.

mHorizontalSpacing and mVerticalSpacing are read from custom attributes. If they're not present, use default values.

```
            R.styleable.CascadeLayout_horizontal_spacing,
            getResources().getDimensionPixelSize(
                R.dimen.cascade_horizontal_spacing));

        mVerticalSpacing = a.getDimensionPixelSize(
            R.styleable.CascadeLayout_vertical_spacing,
                getResources()
                .getDimensionPixelSize(
                    R.dimen.cascade_vertical_spacing));
    } finally {
      a.recycle();
    }

}

...
```

Before coding the onMeasure() method, we'll create a custom LayoutParams. This
class will hold the x,y position values of each child. We'll have the LayoutParams class
as a CascadeLayout inner class. The class definition is as follows:

```
public static class LayoutParams extends ViewGroup.LayoutParams {
  int x;
  int y;

  public LayoutParams(Context context, AttributeSet attrs) {
    super(context, attrs);
  }

  public LayoutParams(int w, int h) {
    super(w, h);
  }
}
```

To use our new CascadeLayout.LayoutParams class, we'll need to override some
additional methods in the CascadeLayout class. These are checkLayoutParams(),
generateDefaultLayoutParams(), generateLayoutParams(AttributeSet attrs),
and generateLayoutParams(ViewGroup.LayoutParams p). The code for these methods is almost always the same between ViewGroups. If you're interested in its content,
you'll find it in the sample code.

The next step is to code the onMeasure() method. This is the key part of the class.
The code follows:

```
@Override
protected void onMeasure(int widthMeasureSpec, int heightMeasureSpec) {
  int width = 0;
  int height = getPaddingTop();

  final int count = getChildCount();
  for (int i = 0; i < count; i++) {
    View child = getChildAt(i);

    measureChild(child, widthMeasureSpec, heightMeasureSpec);

    LayoutParams lp = (LayoutParams) child.getLayoutParams();
    width = getPaddingLeft() + mHorizontalSpacing * i;
```

**Use width and height to
calculate layout's final
size and children's x and
y positions.**

**Make
every
child
measure
itself.**

```
        lp.x = width;
        lp.y = height;

        width += child.getMeasuredWidth();
        height += mVerticalSpacing;
    }

    width += getPaddingRight();
    height += getChildAt(getChildCount() - 1).getMeasuredHeight()
        + getPaddingBottom();

    setMeasuredDimension(resolveSize(width, widthMeasureSpec),
            resolveSize(height, heightMeasureSpec));

}
```

Inside the LayoutParams, hold x and y positions for each child.

Uses calculated width and height to set measured dimensions of whole layout.

The last step is to create the onLayout() method. Let's look at the code:

```
@Override
protected void onLayout(boolean changed, int l, int t, int r, int b) {

    final int count = getChildCount();
    for (int i = 0; i < count; i++) {
        View child = getChildAt(i);
        LayoutParams lp = (LayoutParams) child.getLayoutParams();

        child.layout(lp.x, lp.y, lp.x + child.getMeasuredWidth(), lp.y
            + child.getMeasuredHeight());
    }
}
```

As you can see, the code is dead simple. It calls each child layout() method using the values calculated inside the onMeasure() method.

3.3 *Adding custom attributes to the children*

In this last section, you'll learn how to add custom attributes to the children views. As an example, we'll add a way to override the vertical spacing for a particular child. You can see a result of this in figure 3.3.

The first thing we'll need to do is add a new attribute to the attrs.xml file:

```
<declare-styleable name="CascadeLayout_LayoutParams">
    <attr name="layout_vertical_spacing" format="dimension" />
</declare-styleable>
```

Because the attribute name starts with layout_ instead of containing a View attribute, it's added to the LayoutParams attributes. We'll read this new attribute inside the LayoutParams constructor as we did with the ones from CascadeLayout. The code is the following:

```
public LayoutParams(Context context, AttributeSet attrs) {
    super(context, attrs);

    TypedArray a = context.obtainStyledAttributes(attrs,
        R.styleable.CascadeLayout_LayoutParams);
    try {
        verticalSpacing = a.getDimensionPixelSize(
```

```
        R.styleable.CascadeLayout_LayoutParams_layout_vertical_spacing,
        -1);
  } finally {
    a.recycle();
  }
}
```

The verticalSpacing is a public field. We'll use it inside the CascadeLayout's onMeasure() method. If the child's LayoutParams contains the verticalSpacing, we can use it. The source code looks like the following:

```
verticalSpacing = mVerticalSpacing;

...

LayoutParams lp = (LayoutParams) child.getLayoutParams();

if (lp.verticalSpacing >= 0) {
  verticalSpacing = lp.verticalSpacing;
}

...

width += child.getMeasuredWidth();
height += verticalSpacing;
```

3.4   *The bottom line*

Using custom Views and ViewGroups is an excellent way to organize your application layouts. Customizing components will also allow you to provide custom behaviors. The next time you need to create a complex layout, decide whether or not it'd be better to use a custom ViewGroup. It might be more work at the outset, but the end result is worth it.

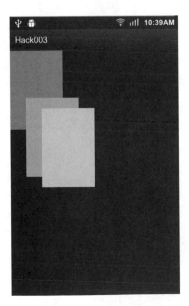

Figure 3.3   First child with different vertical spacing

3.5   *External links*

http://developer.android.com/guide/topics/ui/how-android-draws.html

http://developer.android.com/reference/android/view/ViewGroup.html

http://developer.android.com/reference/android/view/ViewGroup.LayoutParams.html

Hack 4   *Preferences hacks*
Android v1.6+

One of the features I like about the Android SDK is the preferences framework. I prefer it to the iOS SDK because it makes it easier to create layouts. When you edit a simple XML file, you get an easy-to-use preferences screen.

Although Android provides many settings widgets for you to use, sometimes you may need to customize the view. In this hack, you'll find a couple of examples in which the settings framework has been customized. The finished preferences screen is shown in figure 4.1.

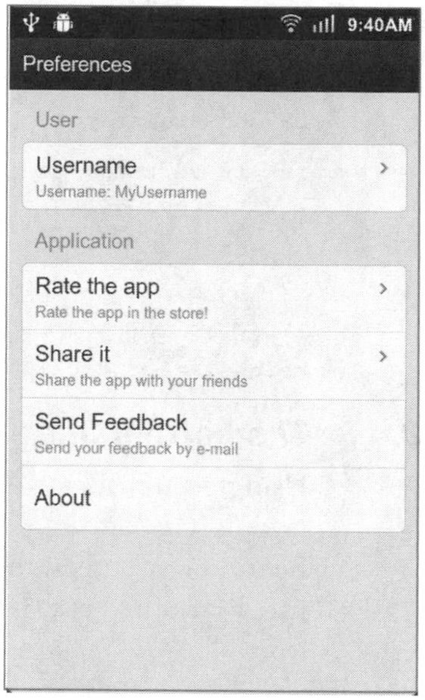

Figure 4.1   Preferences screen

Let's first take a look at the XML:

```xml
<?xml version="1.0" encoding="utf-8"?>
<PreferenceScreen
    xmlns:android="http://schemas.android.com/apk/res/android"
    android:key="pref_first_preferencescreen_key"
    android:title="Preferences">

    <PreferenceCategory
        android:title="User">

        <EditTextPreference
            android:key="pref_username"
            android:summary="Username"
            android:title="Username"/>

    </PreferenceCategory>

    <PreferenceCategory
        android:title="Application">

        <Preference
            android:key="pref_rate"
            android:summary="Rate the app in the store!"
            android:title="Rate the app"/>
```

It's good practice to give preferences an android:key. With that key we're able to retrieve the preferences object.

We can use a PreferenceCategory to separate preferences by certain group names.

To pick a username, we'll use an EditTextPreference. A summary is set, but we'll replace it with the username the user picked.

We'll use a Preference for options that will launch an Intent.

```
<Preference
    android:key="pref_share"
    android:summary="Share this app with your friends"
    android:title="Share it"/>

<com.manning.androidhacks.hack004.preference.EmailDialog
    android:dialogIcon="@drawable/ic_launcher"
    android:dialogTitle="Send Feedback"
    android:dialogMessage="Do you want to send an email?"
    android:key="pref_sendemail_key"
    android:negativeButtonText="Cancel"
    android:positiveButtonText="OK"
    android:summary="Send your feedback by e-mail"
    android:title="Send Feedback"/>

<com.manning.androidhacks.hack004.preference.AboutDialog
    android:dialogIcon="@drawable/ic_launcher"
    android:dialogTitle="About"
    android:key="pref_about_key"
    android:negativeButtonText="@null"
    android:title="About"/>
```

Inside preferences, we can also create custom preferences to extend one of the existing widgets.

```
        </PreferenceCategory>

</PreferenceScreen>
```

The XML we've created will take care of the UI. Now it's time to add all of the logic. To do this, we'll create an `Activity`, but instead of extending `android.app.Activity`, we'll extend `android.preference.PreferenceActivity`. The code follows:

```
public class MainActivity extends PreferenceActivity implements
    OnSharedPreferenceChangeListener {

  @Override
  public void onCreate(Bundle savedInstanceState) {
    super.onCreate(savedInstanceState);
    addPreferencesFromResource(R.xml.prefs);

    ...

    Preference ratePref = findPreference("pref_rate");
    Uri uri = Uri.parse("market://details?id=" + getPackageName());
    Intent goToMarket = new Intent(Intent.ACTION_VIEW, uri);
    ratePref.setIntent(goToMarket);
  }

  @Override
  protected void onResume() {
    super.onResume();


    getPreferenceScreen().getSharedPreferences()
        .registerOnSharedPreferenceChangeListener(this);
  }

  @Override
  protected void onPause() {
    super.onPause();
```

Instead of calling setContentView(), we need to call addPreferences-FromResource with XML we created previously.

In onCreate() method, we can start getting preferences without actions and start setting their Intents. In this case, rate preference will use Intent.ACTION_VIEW.

Register to be notified of preferences changes.

```
    getPreferenceScreen().getSharedPreferences()
        .unregisterOnSharedPreferenceChangeListener(this);        ◁──  Unregister to
  }                                                                     preferences
                                                                        changes.
@Override
public void onSharedPreferenceChanged(
    SharedPreferences sharedPreferences, String key) {

  if (key.equals("pref_username")) {                 ◁──   When there's a change in
    updateUserText();                                       username preference, we
  }                                                         need to update preference
}                                                           summary.

private void updateUserText() {
  EditTextPreference pref;
  pref = (EditTextPreference) findPreference("pref_username");       ◁──
  String user = pref.getText();

  if (user == null) {                      To update summary, we need to get
    user = "?";                            preference and update summary using
  }                                        EditTextPreference's getText() method.

  pref.setSummary(String.format("Username: %s", user));
 }
}
```

The code we want to create shows how to create custom preferences. It works as if we were creating a custom view. To understand it, let's look at the following, where we create the code for the EmailDialog class:

```
public class EmailDialog extends DialogPreference {      ◁──  Custom class should
  Context mContext;                                            extend some of existing
                                                               preferences widgets. In
  public EmailDialog(Context context) {                       this case, we'll use
    this(context, null);                                       DialogPreference.
  }

  public EmailDialog(Context context, AttributeSet attrs) {
    this(context, attrs, 0);
  }

  public EmailDialog(Context context, AttributeSet attrs,
    int defStyle) {                        ◁──

    super(context, attrs, defStyle);              Constructors are the same
    mContext = context;                           as those used to create a
  }                                                custom view extending the
                                                  View class.
  @Override


  public void onClick(DialogInterface dialog, int which) {   ◁──  onClick() is
    super.onClick(dialog, which);                                 overridden. If
                                                                  users press OK
    if (DialogInterface.BUTTON_POSITIVE == which) {               button, then we'll
      LaunchEmailUtil.launchEmailToIntent(mContext);              launch email Intent
    }                                                             with helper class.
  }
}
```

4.1 The bottom line

Although the settings framework allows you to add some custom behavior, you need to remember that its purpose is to create simple preferences screens. If you're thinking of adding more complex user interfaces or flows, I'd recommend you create a separate `Activity`, theming it as a `Dialog`, and launching it from a preferences widget.

4.2 External links

http://developer.android.com/reference/android/preference/PreferenceActivity.html

Creating cool animations

In this chapter, you'll learn about animations. You'll find different examples that use a variety of APIs to add animations to your application widgets.

Hack 5 *Snappy transitions with TextSwitcher and ImageSwitcher*
Android v1.6+

Imagine you need to cycle through information in a `TextView` or in an `ImageView`. Some examples of this would be

- Navigating through a list of dates with Left and Right buttons
- Changing numbers in a date picker
- Countdown clock
- News headlines

Changing the contents of a view is a basic function of most applications, but it doesn't have to be boring. If we use the default `TextView`, you'll notice there's no eye candy when we swap its content. It'd be nice to have a way to apply different animations to content being swapped. So to make our transitions more visually appealing, Android provides two classes called `TextSwitcher` and `ImageSwitcher`. `TextSwitcher` replaces a `TextView` and `ImageSwitcher` replaces an `ImageView`.

TextView and TextSwitcher work in a similar way. Suppose we're navigating through a list of dates, as mentioned earlier. Every time the user clicks a button, we need to change a TextView's content with each date. If we use a TextView, we're swapping out some text in a view using mTextView.setText("something"). Our code should look something like the following:

```
private TextView mTextView;

@Override
public void onCreate(Bundle savedInstanceState) {
  super.onCreate(savedInstanceState);
  mTextView = (TextView) findViewById(R.id.your_textview);

  ...

  mTextView.setText("something");
}
```

As you might've noticed, if we change the content of a TextView, it'll change instantly; TextSwitcher is what we need if we want to add an animation to avoid the hard swap. A TextSwitcher is useful to animate a label onscreen. Whenever it's called, TextSwitcher animates the current text out and animates the new text in. We can get a more pleasant transition by following these easy steps:

1 Get the view using findViewById(), or construct it in your code like any normal Android view.
2 Set a factory using switcher.setFactory().
3 Set an in-animation using switcher.setInAnimation().
4 Set an out-animation using switcher.setOutAnimation().

Here's how TextSwitcher works: it uses the factory to create new views, and whenever we use setText(), it first removes the old view using an animation set with the setOutAnimation() method, and then places the new one using the animation set by the setInAnimation() method. So let's see how to use it:

```
private TextSwitcher mTextSwitcher;

@Override
public void onCreate(Bundle savedInstanceState) {
  super.onCreate(savedInstanceState);
  setContentView(R.layout.main);
  Animation in = AnimationUtils.loadAnimation(this,
    android.R.anim.fade_in);
  Animation out = AnimationUtils.loadAnimation(this,
    android.R.anim.fade_out);

  mTextSwitcher = (TextSwitcher) findViewById(R.id.your_textview);
  mTextSwitcher.setFactory(new ViewFactory() {

    @Override
    public View makeView() {
      TextView t = new TextView(YourActivity.this);
      t.setGravity(Gravity.CENTER);
```

```
        return t;
      }
  }));

  mTextSwitcher.setInAnimation(in);
  mTextSwitcher.setOutAnimation(out);
}
```

That's it. The user gets the new text, and we get some cool animations for free. The new transition fades out the original text while the new text fades in to replace it. Because we used android.R.anim.fade_in in our example, the effect was a fade-in. This technique works equally well with other effects. Providing your own animation or using one from android.R.anim. ImageSwitcher works in the same way, except with images instead of text.

5.1   The bottom line

The TextSwitcher and ImageSwitcher methods give you a simple way to add animated transitions. Their role is to make these transitions less dull and more vibrant. Don't abuse them; you don't want your application to look like a Christmas tree!

5.2   External links

http://developer.android.com/reference/android/widget/TextSwitcher.html
http://developer.android.com/guide/topics/graphics/view-animation.html

Hack 6   *Adding eye candy to your ViewGroup's children*
Android v1.6+

By default, when you add views to a ViewGroup, they're instantly added and displayed, but there's an easier way to animate that action. In this hack, I'll show you how to apply an animation to children views being added to their parent ViewGroup. I'll show you how to add eye candy to your application in a few lines.

Android provides a class called LayoutAnimationController. This class is useful to animate a layout's or a ViewGroup's children. It's important to mention that you won't be able to provide different animations for each child, but the LayoutAnimation-Controller can help you decide when the animation should apply to each child.

The best way to understand how to use LayoutAnimationController is through an example. We'll animate ListView's children with a mix of two animations, alpha and translate. You can use the LayoutAnimationController in two ways: from the code and from the XML. I'll show how to do it from code and you can try converting it to XML as an exercise. Let's look at the code used to apply the animation:

```
mListView = (ListView) findViewById(R.id.my_listview_id);          ◁──── ❶ Get
                                                                          ListView ref.
AnimationSet set = new AnimationSet(true);

Animation animation = new AlphaAnimation(0.0f, 1.0f);    ◁──── ❸ Create alpha
animation.setDuration(50);                                       animation.
set.addAnimation(animation);

animation = new TranslateAnimation(Animation.RELATIVE_TO_SELF, 0.0f,
  Animation.RELATIVE_TO_SELF, 0.0f, Animation.RELATIVE_TO_SELF,
  -1.0f, Animation.RELATIVE_TO_SELF, 0.0f);
animation.setDuration(100);                              ◁──── ❹ Create translate
set.addAnimation(animation);                                    animation.

LayoutAnimationController controller = new LayoutAnimationController(
  set, 0.5f);
                                              ◁──── ❺ Create LayoutAnimationController
mListView.setLayoutAnimation(controller);            and delay between animations.
```

Create set and use default. ❷

Apply Layout-Animation-Controller. ❻

First, you need to get the ListView reference ❶. Because we want to add more than one animation, we'll need to use a set ❷. The Boolean variable will determine whether every animation will use the same interpolator. In this example, we'll use the default interpolator, and then create the alpha animation ❸ and the translate animation ❹, and add them to the set. We create the LayoutAnimationController with the set and the delay between child animations ❺. Finally, we apply the Layout-AnimationController to the ListView ❻.

Most of the animations provided by the framework look like TranslateAnimation, so let's take a closer look at that particular code. The constructor is defined as follows:

```
public TranslateAnimation(int fromXType, float fromXValue, int toXType,
  float toXValue, int fromYType, float fromYValue, int toYType,
  float toYValue) {
```

The idea is simple: we need to provide initial and final x,y coordinates. Android provides a way to specify where it should calculate the position from, with three options:

- Animation.ABSOLUTE
- Animation.RELATIVE_TO_SELF
- Animation.RELATIVE_TO_PARENT

If we go back to our example, we can explain every child position with words like this:

- Initial X: Position provided by its parent
- Initial Y: -1 from the position provided by its parent
- Final X: Position provided by its parent
- Final Y: Position provided by its parent

The end result will be every child "falling" through the y axis to its position. Because we have a delay between children, it'll look like a cascade.

6.1 **The bottom line**

Adding animations to ViewGroups is easy and they make your application look professional and polished. This hack only covered a small portion of what you can do, but, for example, you can try changing the default interpolator to the BounceInterpolator. This will make your views bounce when they reach their final position. You can also change the order in which to animate the children.

Use your imagination to create something cool, but don't overdo it—you should avoid using too many animations.

6.2 **External links**

http://developer.android.com/reference/android/view/animation/
LayoutAnimationController.html

Hack 7 *Doing animations over the Canvas*
Android v1.6+

If you're animating your own widgets, you might find the animation APIs a bit limited. Is there an Android API to draw things directly to the screen? The answer is yes. Android offers a class called Canvas.

In this hack, I'll show you how to use the Canvas class to draw elements and animate them by creating a box that will bounce around the screen. You can see the finished application in figure 7.1.

Before we create this application, let's make sure you understand what the Canvas class is—the following is from the documentation (see section 7.2):

> A Canvas works for you as a pretense, or interface, to the actual surface upon which your graphics will be drawn—it holds all of your "draw" calls. Via the Canvas, your drawing is performed upon an underlying Bitmap, which is placed into the window.

Based on that definition, the Canvas class holds all of the draw calls. We can create a View, override the onDraw() method, and start drawing primitives there.

To make everything more clear, we'll create a DrawView class that will take care of drawing the box

Figure 7.1 Box bouncing around the screen

and updating its position. Because we don't have anything else onscreen, we'll make it the `Activity`'s content view. The following is the code for the `Activity`:

```
public class MainActivity extends Activity {

  private DrawView mDrawView;

  @Override
  public void onCreate(Bundle savedInstanceState) {
    super.onCreate(savedInstanceState);

    Display display = getWindowManager().getDefaultDisplay();
    mDrawView = new DrawView(this);
    mDrawView.height = display.getHeight();
    mDrawView.width = display.getWidth();

    setContentView(mDrawView);
  }
}
```

❶ Get the screen width and height.

❷ DrawView takes all the available space.

We'll use the `WindowManager` to get the screen width and height ❶. These values will be used inside the `DrawView` to limit where to draw. Afterward, we'll set the `DrawView` as the `Activity`'s `contentView` ❷. This means that the `DrawView` will take all of the available space.

Let's take a look at what's happening inside the `DrawView` class:

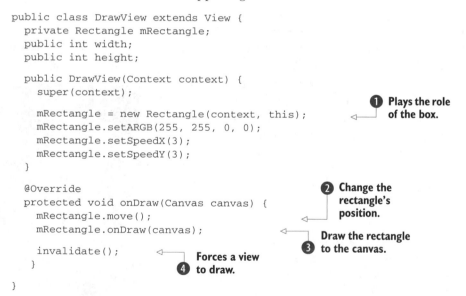

```
public class DrawView extends View {
  private Rectangle mRectangle;
  public int width;
  public int height;

  public DrawView(Context context) {
    super(context);

    mRectangle = new Rectangle(context, this);
    mRectangle.setARGB(255, 255, 0, 0);
    mRectangle.setSpeedX(3);
    mRectangle.setSpeedY(3);
  }

  @Override
  protected void onDraw(Canvas canvas) {
    mRectangle.move();
    mRectangle.onDraw(canvas);

    invalidate();
  }
}
```

❶ Plays the role of the box.

❷ Change the rectangle's position.

❸ Draw the rectangle to the canvas.

❹ Forces a view to draw.

We'll first create a `Rectangle` instance that will play the role of the box ❶. The `Rectangle` class also knows how to draw itself to a canvas and contains all of the boring logic regarding how to update its position to be drawn in the correct place. When the `onDraw()` method gets called, we'll change the rectangle's position ❷ and draw it to the canvas ❸. The `invalidate()` call ❹ is the hack itself. The `invalidate()` call is a `View`'s method to force a view to draw. Placing it inside the `onDraw()` method means that `onDraw()` will be called as soon as the view finishes drawing itself. To put it differently, we're looping over the `Rectangle`'s `move()` and `onDraw()` calls to create a nice animation.

7.1 The bottom line

Updating view positions in the `onDraw()` method through the `invalidate()` call is an easy way to provide custom animations. If you're planning to make a small game, using this trick is a simple way to handle your game's main loop.

7.2 External links

http://developer.android.com/reference/android/graphics/Canvas.html
http://developer.android.com/guide/topics/graphics/2d-graphics.html

Hack 8   *Slideshow using the Ken Burns effect*
Android v1.6+

One of the first products my company created is called FeedTV. The idea behind FeedTV is to change the way we read RSS feeds. Instead of showing them in a long list, we created something like a photo frame application that shows the feed's headline and its main image. FeedTV for the iPad can be seen in figure 8.1.

Figure 8.1   FeedTV running in an iPad

To make it even cooler, instead of placing a still image, we'll analyze the image and, using it's size and aspect ratio, apply something called the *Ken Burns effect*. The Ken Burns effect is nothing more than a type of panning and zooming effect used in video production from still imagery. The best way to understand the Ken Burns effect is to watch a video, but figure 8.2 can also give you an idea of how it works.

Figure 8.2   Ken Burns effect example taken from Wikipedia

In this hack, I'll show you how to mimic the Ken Burns effect in an image slideshow. To do this, we'll use a library created by Jake Wharton called Nine Old Androids. The Nine Old Androids library lets you use the new Android 3.0 animation API in older versions.

To create the Ken Burns effect, we'll have a number of preset animations. These animations will be applied randomly to an ImageView and, when the animation is finished, we'll start another animation with the next photo. The main layout will be a FrameLayout, and we'll place ImageViews inside it. The layout is created with the following code:

```
@Override
public void onCreate(Bundle savedInstanceState) {
  super.onCreate(savedInstanceState);

  mContainer = new FrameLayout(this);
  mContainer.setLayoutParams(new LayoutParams(          ◁── Create container.
    LayoutParams.FILL_PARENT, LayoutParams.FILL_PARENT));

  mView = createNewView();
  mContainer.addView(mView);                    ◁── Create and add ImageView.

  setContentView(mContainer);
}

private ImageView createNewView() {
  ImageView ret = new ImageView(this);
  ret.setLayoutParams(new LayoutParams(LayoutParams.FILL_PARENT,
  LayoutParams.FILL_PARENT));
  ret.setScaleType(ScaleType.FIT_XY);                    Set image to show
  ret.setImageResource(PHOTOS[mIndex]);          ◁──┘  and increment index.
  mIndex = (mIndex + 1 < PHOTOS.length) ? mIndex + 1 : 0;

  return ret;
}
```

So far, so good. We'll use the createNewView() to create new ImageViews and keep track of the image we're showing next. The next step is to create a method called nextAnimation(). This method will take care of setting the animation and start it. The code follows:

```
private void nextAnimation() {
  AnimatorSet anim = new AnimatorSet();
  final int index = mRandom.nextInt(ANIM_COUNT);     ◁── Pick animation randomly.

  switch (index) {
    case 0:
      anim.playTogether(                                   Scaling
        ObjectAnimator.ofFloat(mView, "scaleX", 1.5f, 1f),   ◁──┘ animation.
        ObjectAnimator.ofFloat(mView, "scaleY", 1.5f, 1f));
      break;

    ...
```

```
    case 3:
    default:
      AnimatorProxy.wrap(mView).setScaleX(1.5f);
      AnimatorProxy.wrap(mView).setScaleY(1.5f);
      anim.playTogether(ObjectAnimator.ofFloat(mView,
        "translationX", 0f, 40f));
    break;
  }

  anim.setDuration(3000);
  anim.addListener(this);
  anim.start();
}
```

❶ Translation animation

❷ Set the duration, set Activity as listener, and start it.

The `AnimatorProxy` ❶ is a class available in the Nine Old Androids library to modify `View`'s properties. The new animation framework is based on the possibility of modifying `View`'s properties over time. The `AnimatorProxy` is used because on Android versions lower than 3.0 some properties had no getters/setters.

The remaining code is calling the `nextAnimation()` method when the animation is finished. Remember, we set the `Activity` as the animation listener ❷? Let's look at the overridden method:

```
@Override
public void onAnimationEnd(Animator animator) {
  mContainer.removeView(mView);
  mView = createNewView();
  mContainer.addView(mView);

  nextAnimation();
}
```

Remove old view from container and add new one.

Start new animation.

That's it. We have our Ken Burns effect running on every photo. You can try improving the sample by doing two things: adding an alpha animation when switching views and adding an `AnimationSet` that pans and zooms at the same time. You can get additional ideas from the Nine Old Androids sample code.

8.1 The bottom line

The new animation API has better potential than the previous one. Following is a short list of improvements:

- Previous version supported animations only on `View` objects
- Previous version limited to move, rotate, scale, and fade
- Previous version changed the visual appearance, not the real position, in the case of a move

The fact that a library like Nine Old Androids exists means there's no excuse for not trying it out on the new API.

8.2   *External links*

www.nasatrainedmonkeys.com/portfolio/feedtv/

https://github.com/JakeWharton/NineOldAndroids

http://en.wikipedia.org/wiki/Ken_Burns_effect

http://android-developers.blogspot.com.ar/2011/02/animation-in-honeycomb.html

http://android-developers.blogspot.com.ar/2011/05/
   introducing-viewpropertyanimator.html

View tips and tricks

3

In this chapter, you'll read about different hacks that use views. Most of them show how to customize and/or tweak widgets to perform certain functionalities.

Hack 9 *Avoiding date validations with an EditText for dates*
Android v1.6+

We all know that validating data in forms is boring as well as error-prone. I worked on an Android application that used a lot of forms and had a couple of date inputs. I didn't want to validate the date fields, so I found an elegant way to avoid it. The idea is to make users think they have an EditText when it's in fact a button that will show a DatePicker when clicked.

To make this happen, we'll change the default background of an Android Button to the EditText's background. We can do this easily from the XML:

```
<Button android:id="@+id/details_date"
    android:layout_width="wrap_content"
    android:layout_height="wrap_content"
    android:gravity="center_vertical"
    android:background="@android:drawable/edit_text" />
```

Note how we used @android:drawable instead of a drawable of our own. Using Android's resources inside your application has its pros and cons. It makes your application fit in the device, but it'll look different on different devices. Some developers prefer using their own resources, drawables, and themes to have their own look.

If you've been testing your application in different devices, you'll notice that widgets might not have the same styles. Using Android's resources will make your application maintain Android's styles.

After creating the button, we need to set its click listener. It should look something like the following:

```
mDate = (Button) findViewById(R.id.details_date);
mDate.setOnClickListener(new OnClickListener() {

    @Override
    public void onClick(View v) {
        showDialog(DATE_DIALOG_ID);
    }
});
```

The rest of the code sets up the DatePicker and sets the text into the Button after the user has picked a date.

9.1   The bottom line

You might be asking yourself why we didn't set a click listener to the EditText instead of using a Button. Using a Button is safer because the user won't be able to modify the text. If you used an EditText and only set the click listener, the user could gain focus by using the arrow and modifying the text without going through your picker.

You can always use a TextWatcher with your EditText to validate user input, but it's boring and it takes a lot of time. Using this hack means less coding and avoiding user input errors. Remember that using Android's resources is a good way to use the device's styles inside your application.

9.2   External links

http://developer.android.com/reference/android/widget/DatePicker.html
http://developer.android.com/reference/android/widget/EditText.html

Hack 10 *Formatting a TextView's text*
Android v1.6+

Imagine a Twitter application showing a tweet (see figure 10.1). Note the different text styles within it. You might think that Twitter created a new custom view, but the widget used is a TextView.

Sometimes you'll want to add text with different styles to show emphasis or provide visual feedback on ░░░░ ░░░░ ░░░░ ░░░░ ░░░░ ░░░░ ░░░░ ░░░░ Other examples of where it's useful to use text styles include these:

Figure 10.1   Twitter example

- Showing links for the telephone field
- Using a different background color for different parts of the text

In this hack, I'll show how the TextView helps us add styled text and links.

The first thing we'll add is the hyperlink. We can set a TextView's text using Html.fromHtml(). The idea is simple: we'll use HTML for the TextView's text. Here's the code:

```
mTextView1 = (TextView) findViewById(R.id.my_text_view_html);
String text =
    "Visit <a href=\"http://manning.com/\">Manning home page</a>";
mTextView1.setText(Html.fromHtml(text));
mTextView1.setMovementMethod(LinkMovementMethod.getInstance());
```

Using HTML to set styles in a TextView is fine, but what does the Html.fromHtml() method do? What does it return? It converts HTML into a Spanned object to use with a TextView's setText() method.

Now we'll try something different. Instead of using HTML to format the text, we'll create a Spanned object using the SpannableString class. Here's the source code:

```
mTextView2 = (TextView) findViewById(R.id.my_text_view_spannable);
Spannable sText = new SpannableString(mTextView2.getText());
sText.setSpan(new BackgroundColorSpan(Color.RED), 1, 4, 0);
sText.setSpan(new ForegroundColorSpan(Color.BLUE), 5, 9, 0);
mTextView2.setText(sText);
```

We can see the visual output of both examples in figure 10.2. The idea is simple: we add different spans using different indexes inside the text. Using a SpannableString, we can place different styles in different parts of the text.

10.1   The bottom line

Android's TextView is a simple but powerful widget. You can use styled texts in different ways inside your application. Although TextView doesn't support all the HTML tags, they're enough to format the text nicely. Try it out.

Visit Manning home page
Hello World, HomeActivity!

Figure 10.2   TextView using spannables

10.2   External links

http://developer.android.com/reference/android/widget/TextView.html

Hack 11   *Adding text glowing effects*
Android v1.6+

Imagine you need to create an application that shows the time. Do you remember those digital clocks that displayed a super-bright green light? In this hack, I'll show you how to tweak Android's `TextView` to generate that exact effect. The final image we're after can be seen in figure 11.1.

Figure 11.1   Digital clock demo

The first thing we'll do is create an `LedTextView` class that extends `TextView`. This class will be used to set a specific font, which makes the text look like it was written in LEDs (light-emitting diodes). Let's look at the code:

```
public class LedTextView extends TextView {

  public LedTextView(Context context, AttributeSet attrs) {
    super(context, attrs);

    AssetManager assets = context.getAssets();
    final Typeface font = Typeface.createFromAsset(assets,
        FONT_DIGITAL_7);
    setTypeface(font);
  }
}
```
❶ Sets the typeface

When the object is created, we get the font from the assets folder and set it as the typeface ❶. Now that we have a widget capable of showing text with a custom font, we'll take care of how the numbers will be drawn. If you check figure 11.1 you'll notice it can be done with two `TextViews`. The first one is a shadow in the back that draws 88:88:88, and the second one draws the current time.

To add the glowing effect, the `TextView` provides a method with the following signature:

```
public void setShadowLayer (float radius, float dx, float dy, int color)
```

This can also be accessed from the XML with the following properties: `android:shadowColor`, `android:shadowDx`, `android:shadowDy`, and `android:shadowRadius`.

Let's take a look on how we can apply it:

```
<?xml version="1.0" encoding="utf-8"?>
<RelativeLayout
    xmlns:android="http://schemas.android.com/apk/res/android"
    android:orientation="vertical"
    android:layout_width="fill_parent"
    android:layout_height="fill_parent">

    <com.manning.androidhacks.hack011.view.LedTextView
        android:layout_width="wrap_content"
        android:layout_height="wrap_content"
        android:layout_centerInParent="true"
        android:text="88:88:88"
        android:textSize="80sp"
```

```
        android:textColor="#3300FF00"/>

    <com.manning.androidhacks.hack011.view.LedTextView
        android:id="@+id/.............................."
        android:layout_width="wrap_content"
        android:layout_height="wrap_content"
        android:layout_centerInParent="true"
        android:text="08:43:02"
        android:textSize="80sp"
        android:textColor="#00FF00"
        android:shadowColor="#00FF00"
        android:shadowDx="0"
        android:shadowDy="0"
        android:shadowRadius="10"/>
```

1 Sets color to be transparent

2 Text color, shadow color are same

3 Modifies shadow radius to look brighter

```
</RelativeLayout>
```

The first LedTextView draws the 88:88:88 in the back. The purpose of this view is mocking the ghosting effect in old digital clocks. We've achieved that look by setting the text color to be a bit transparent **1**. The second LedTextView shows the current time. Note that the text color and the shadow color are the same **2**. We could've played with the alpha as well.

Modifying the android:shadowDx and android:shadowDy values differentiates the shadow position from the text position. The shadow radius will give the sensation of the text being brighter. To create the glowing effect, we didn't use the android:shadowDx or android:shadowDy properties, but we modified the shadow radius to make it look brighter **3**.

11.1 The bottom line

Making your application look great is the best way to get good reviews in the market. Sometimes, polishing your widgets takes a few more lines of code, but they're worth it. In addition, using shadows in texts is simple and will make your views look professional. Try it out. You won't regrct it.

11.2 External links

http://www.styleseven.com/php/get_product.php?product=Digital-7
http://developer.android.com/reference/android/widget/TextView.html

Hack 12 *Rounded borders for backgrounds*
Android v1.6+

When you pick a background for your application's widgets, you typically use images. In general, you want to avoid the default styles, adding your own colors and shapes.

Rounded borders are a feature you can add to your application that looks nice, using only a few lines of code.

As an example, let's add a gray `Button` with rounded corners to the Hello World demonstration. What we'll create is shown in figure 12.1.

Hello World, MainActivity!

Figure 12.1   `Button` **with rounded corners**

For this, we'll add a `Button` to the layout using the following XML:

```
<Button android:layout_width="wrap_content"
    android:layout_height="wrap_content"
    android:text="@string/hello"
    android:textColor="#000000"
    android:padding="10dp"
    android:background="@drawable/button_rounded_background"/>
```

As you can see, we didn't add any strange properties. A `drawable` is assigned as a background, but it's not an image, it's an XML file. In the `drawable`'s XML resides a `Shape-Drawable` object. A `ShapeDrawable` is a drawable object that creates primitive shapes such as rectangles. Here's the XML for the `ShapeDrawable`:

```
<shape xmlns:android="http://schemas.android.com/apk/res/android"
    android:shape="rectangle">
    <solid android:color="#AAAAAA"/>
    <corners android:radius="15dp"/>
</shape>
```

Apart from the radius, we defined a shape and solid color. These aren't the only available properties; you can read the documentation (section 12.2) and see what else is available for `ShapeDrawables`.

12.1   The bottom line

The `ShapeDrawable` is a nice tool to add effects to your widgets. This trick works for every widget that can have a background. You can also try using it with `ListViews` to make your applications look more professional.

12.2   External links

http://developer.android.com/guide/topics/resources/drawable-resource.html#Shape

Hack 13   *Getting the view's width and height in the onCreate() method*
Android v1.6+

When you want to do something that depends on a widget's width and height, you might want to use `View`'s `getHeight()` and `getWidth()` methods. A common pitfall

for new Android developers is trying to get a widget's width and height inside the
`Activity`'s `onCreate()` method. Unfortunately, those methods will return 0 if you call
them from there, but I'll show you an easy way around this.

Let's first see why we get a 0 when we ask for the view's sizes inside the `Activity`'s
`onCreate()` method. When the `onCreate()` method is called, the content view is set
inflating the layout XML with a `LayoutInflater`. The process of inflation involves creating the views but not setting their sizes. So when does the view get assigned its size?
Let's review what the Android documentation (see section 13.2) says:

> Drawing the layout is a two pass process: a measure pass and a
> layout pass. The measuring pass is implemented in `measure(int,
> int)` and is a top-down traversal of the `View` tree. Each `View`
> pushes dimension specifications down the tree during the
> recursion. At the end of the measure pass, every `View` has stored its
> measurements. The second pass happens in `layout(int, int,
> int, int)` and is also top-down. During this pass each parent is
> responsible for positioning all of its children using the sizes
> computed in the measure pass.

The conclusion is the following: `View`s get their height and width when the layout happens. Layout happens after the `onCreate()` method is called, so we get a 0 when we
call `getHeight()` or `getWidth()` from it.

Imagine the XML layout as a cake recipe: the `LayoutInflater` would be the person
in charge of buying all of the items; the bakers would do the measuring and layout of
passes; and the view would be the cake itself. During the `onCreate()` method, the
ingredients will be purchases, but knowing what ingredients make up the cake isn't
enough information to know how big the cake will end up being.

To solve this issue, we can use the `View`'s `post()` method. This method receives a
`Runnable` and adds it to the message queue. An interesting thing is that the `Runnable`
will be executed on the user interface thread. The code to use the `post()` call should
look like the following:

```
protected void onCreate(Bundle savedInstanceState) {
    super.onCreate(savedInstanceState);

    setContentView(R.layout.main);
    View view = findViewById(R.id.main_my_view);        Get size of view
                                                         after layout
    view.post(new Runnable() {

        @Override
        public void run() {                                 Correct width
                                                            and height
            Log.d(TAG, "view has width: "+view.getWidth() +
                " and height: "+view.getHeight());
        }
    });
}
```

13.1 The bottom line

The post() method is used in several parts inside Android itself, and isn't only for getting the width and height of a view. Look at the View class source code and search for the post keyword. You'll be surprised how many times it gets called. Understanding how the framework works is important in avoiding these kinds of pitfalls. As I always say, understand what it's for and don't abuse it.

13.2 External links

http://source.android.com/source/downloading.html
http://developer.android.com/guide/topics/ui/how-android-draws.html

Hack 14 *VideoViews and orientation changes*
Android v1.6+

Adding video to an application is a great way to create a rich user experience. I've seen applications that provide company information using fancy graphs containing videos. Sometimes videos are an easy way to present information in complex views without the need for coding the animation logic.

I noticed that when a video is available, users tend to turn the device to landscape to enjoy it, so in this hack I'll show you how to make the video full-screen when the device is rotated.

To create this, we'll tell the system that we'll handle the orientation changes ourselves. When the device is rotated, we'll change the size and position of the videoView.

The first thing to do is create the layout we want for our Activity. For this hack, I created a layout divided in two by a small line. The upper part will have a small bit of text on the left with a video on the right, and the bottom part will have a long description. When I created the XML for this view, instead of adding a videoView, I added

Figure 14.1   Finished layout

a View with a white background. This view will be used to copy its size and position to place the videoView correctly. You can see the finished layout in figure 14.1.

In figure 14.2 you can see how the view tree is created. The videoView hangs from the root view at the same level as the portrait content. Placing the videoView there will allow us to change its size and position without needing to use two different layouts or changing the videoView's parent when rotation occurs. On the other hand, the white background view, called the *portrait position*, is placed deeper in the tree.

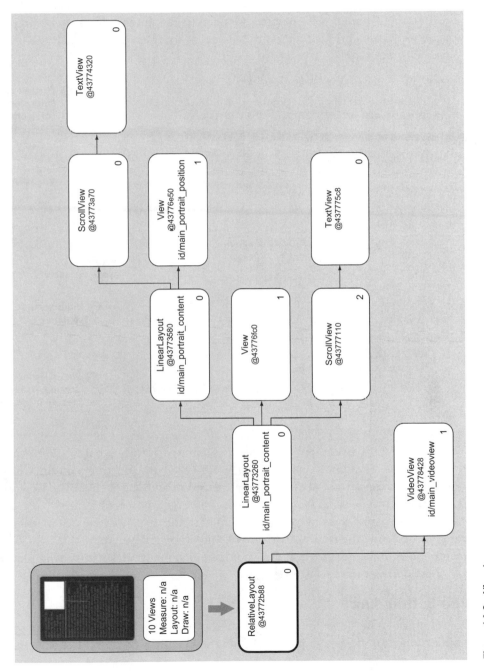

Figure 14.2 View tree

Now that we have the layout, we can take care of the Activity's code. The first thing to do is to enable handling the orientation changes. To do this, we need to add android:configChanges="orientation" to the proper <Activity> element inside AndroidManifest.xml. Adding that attribute will cause the onConfiguration-Changed() method to be called instead of restarting the Activity when the device is rotated.

When the orientation is changed, we need to change the video's size and position. For this we'll call a private method called setVideoViewPosition(). Here's is the content of this method:

```
private void setVideoViewPosition() {

    if (getResources().getConfiguration().orientation ==          ❶ Portrait and
       ActivityInfo.SCREEN_ORIENTATION_PORTRAIT) {                    landscape
                                                                      configurations
       mPortraitContent.setVisibility(View.VISIBLE);

       int[] locationArray = new int[2];                          ❸ videoView
       mPortraitPosition.getLocationOnScreen(locationArray);         position

       RelativeLayout.LayoutParams params =
          new RelativeLayout.LayoutParams(mPortraitPosition.getWidth(),
             mPortraitPosition.getHeight());

       params.leftMargin = locationArray[0];
       params.topMargin = locationArray[1];
                                                                  ❹ Sets videoView's
       mVideoView.setLayoutParams(params);                          layout parameters

    } else {
                                                                  ❺ Hides portrait
       mPortraitContent.setVisibility(View.GONE);                   content

       RelativeLayout.LayoutParams params =
          new RelativeLayout.LayoutParams(LayoutParams.FILL_PARENT,
             LayoutParams.FILL_PARENT);
                                                                  ❻ Shows layout
       params.addRule(RelativeLayout.CENTER_IN_PARENT);             parameters we
       mVideoView.setLayoutParams(params);                          created in videoView
    }
}
```

Makes content visible ❷

The setVideoViewPosition() method is separated into two parts: the portrait and the landscape configurations ❶. First, we'll make the portrait content visible ❷. Because the videoView will have the same position and size as the white view, we want its position ❸ to be set as the videoView's layout parameters ❹.

Something similar is done in the second part, for the landscape orientation. In this case, we first hide the portrait content ❺, and afterward we create the layout parameters to make the videoView use the whole screen. Finally, we set the layout parameters we've created to the videoView ❻.

14.1   The bottom line

As I mentioned at the beginning of this hack, videos can be useful for improving your application content. You should know that the default videoView class will respect the aspect ratio when resizing, and if you wish to make it fill the space available, you'll need to override the onMeasure() method in your own custom view.

14.2 External links

http://developer.android.com/guide/topics/resources/runtime-changes.html

Hack 15   *Removing the background to improve your Activity startup time*
Android v1.6+

Inside the Android SDK, you'll find a tool called Hierarchy Viewer. You can use this tool to detect unused views and lower the view tree height. If you open a view tree inside the tool, you'll see some nodes over which you don't have control. In this hack, we'll look at what these nodes are and see how we can tweak them to improve our Activity startup time.

If we create the default new Android application and run it, we'll see something similar to figure 15.1. When we run the Hierarchy Viewer with this Activity, we'll see something like figure 15.2. We need to diminish the height of the tree.

Figure 15.1   The default Android application

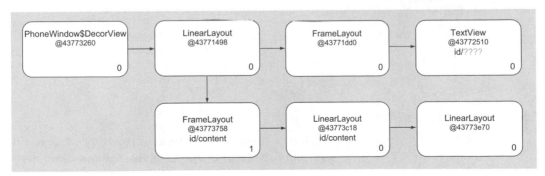

Figure 15.2   Hierarchy Viewer showing the view tree

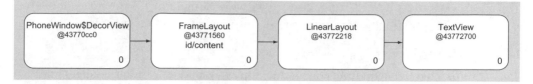

Figure 15.3 Hierarchy Viewer showing the view tree without title

First, let's remove some of the nodes by removing the title. The title is the gray bar on top with the text that reads BackgroundTest, which is formed by a `FrameLayout` and a `TextView`. We can delete these nodes by creating a theme.xml file under the res/values directory with the following content:

```xml
<?xml version="1.0" encoding="utf-8"?>
<resources>
    <style name="Theme.NoBackground" parent="android:Theme">
        <item name="android:windowNoTitle">true</item>
    </style>
</resources>
```

We can apply this theme in our Android manifest by modifying the `<application>` tag and adding `android:theme="@style/Theme.NoBackground"` as an attribute. If we run the application again, the title will disappear and the view tree will look like figure 15.3.

You already know what `LinearLayout` and `TextView` are, but what about `PhoneWindow$DecorView` and `FrameLayout`?

`FrameLayout` is created when we execute the `setContentView()` method, and the `DecorView` is the root of the tree. By default, the framework fills our window with a default background color and the `DecorView` is the view that holds the window's background drawable. So if we have an opaque UI or a custom background, our device is wasting time drawing the default background color.

If we're sure that we'll use opaque user interfaces in our activity, we can remove the default background to boost our startup time. To do this, we need to add a line to the theme mentioned previously, as shown next:

```xml
<?xml version="1.0" encoding="utf-8"?>
<resources>
    <style name="Theme.NoBackground" parent="android:Theme">
        <item name="android:windowNoTitle">true</item>
        <item name="android:windowBackground">@null</item>
    </style>
</resources>
```

15.1 *The bottom line*

Removing the window background is a simple trick to gain some speed. The rule is simple: if the UI of your application is drawing 100% of the window contents, you should always set `windowBackground` to null. Remember that the theme can be set in an `<application>` or an `<activity>` tag.

15.2 *External links*

http://developer.android.com/guide/developing/debugging/
   debugging-ui.html#HierarchyViewer

http://stackoverflow.com/questions/6499004/
   androidwindowbackground-null-to-improve-app-speed

Hack 16 *Toast's position hack*
Android v1.6+

In Android, whenever you need to notify the user that something happened you can use a class called `Toast`. A `Toast` is a pop-up notification that usually shows a text, and it's placed in the bottom middle of the screen. If you've never seen a `Toast`, take a look at figure 16.1. The `Toast` is the black box that says, "This alarm is set for 17 hours and 57 minutes from now."

Figure 16.1 A `Toast` example from the Alarm application

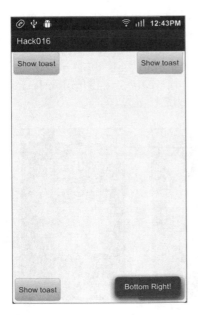

Figure 16.2 `Toast` with different position

The API to launch a `Toast` is super simple. For example, to launch a `Toast` that says, "Hi!" we only need to write the following code:

```
Toast.makeText(this, "Hi!", Toast.LENGTH_SHORT).show();
```

The `Toast` class isn't flexible at all. For example, for the duration parameter we can only pick between `Toast.LENGTH _SHORT` and `Toast.LENGTH_LONG`. Although there aren't many things we can change about `Toast`, what we can change is where the pop-up is placed.

Depending on our application layout, we might want to position the `Toast` somewhere else, for instance, on top of certain views. Let's see how to create a `Toast` so that it's shown in a different position than the default one. A working example can be seen in figure 16.2. In the sample application, we have four bottoms, one on each corner. When a button is clicked, a `Toast` is created and positioned over the corner where the button is located.

To move the `Toast` around the screen, we need to create it a bit differently. It has a public method inside the class with the following signature:

```
public void setGravity(int gravity, int xOffset, int yOffset);
```

To reproduce the `Toast` shown in figure 16.2 we'd need to use the following:

```
Toast toast = Toast.makeText(this, "Bottom Right!",          ◁—— Create Toast
        Toast.LENGTH_SHORT);

    toast.setGravity(Gravity.BOTTOM | Gravity.RIGHT, 0, 0);  ◁— Set gravity to avoid
    toast.show();                                               default position
```

16.1   The bottom line

Although this hack might look simple, many Android developer aren't aware of this solution. You might find changing the position useful when your screen is split into different `Fragment`s and you want the `Toast` to show in a specific place.

16.2   External links

http://developer.android.com/guide/topics/ui/notifiers/toasts.html

Hack 17   *Creating a wizard form using a Gallery*
Android v2.1+

You may find circumstances will arise when you need your users to fill out a long form. Maybe you need to create a registration form, or your application needs some form to upload content. In other platforms, you can create something called a *wizard form*, which is a form separated in different views. But in Android, this type of widget doesn't exist. In this hack, we'll use the `Gallery` widget to create a registration form with many fields. The result we're after is shown in figure 17.1.

Figure 17.1   Wizard form using a Gallery

For the sake of this example, we'll create a registration form where the user will need to fill in the following information:

- Full name
- Email
- Password
- Gender
- City
- Country
- Postal code

We'll have two fields per page, so in total we'll have four pages. To create the wizard form, we need to create an `Activity` called `CreateAccountActivity`. This `Activity` will use a `Theme.Dialog` style to give the form the look and feel of a pop-up. Inside it we'll place a `Gallery`, which will be populated with an `Adapter`. The `Adapter` will need to communicate with the `Activity`, and for that we'll use a `Delegate` interface.

Let's first create the generic view for each page. The XML follows:

```xml
<?xml version="1.0" encoding="utf-8"?>
<RelativeLayout
    xmlns:android="http://schemas.android.com/apk/res/android"
    android:layout_width="270dp"
    android:layout_height="350dp">

    <LinearLayout android:id="@+id/create_account_form"
        android:layout_width="fill_parent"
        android:layout_height="wrap_content"
        android:layout_alignParentTop="true"
        android:orientation="vertical"
        android:paddingLeft="10dp"
        android:paddingTop="10dp"
        android:paddingRight="10dp"
        android:background="#AAAAAA">

        <TextView
            android:layout_width="wrap_content"
            android:layout_height="wrap_content"
            android:text="Account creation"
            android:textColor="#000000"
            android:textStyle="bold"
            android:textSize="20sp"/>

    </LinearLayout>

    <Button
        android:id="@+id/create_account_next"
        android:layout_width="wrap_content"
        android:layout_height="wrap_content"
        android:layout_alignParentTop="true"
        android:layout_alignParentRight="true"
        android:textSize="12sp"
        android:gravity="center"
        android:layout_marginTop="10dp"
```

Inside LinearLayout you place all fields.

At first item of LinearLayout you place form title.

Next button will be used to move forward through wizard pages.

```
        android:layout_marginRight="10dp"
        android:text="Next"/>

    <Button
        android:id="@+id/create_account_create"
        android:layout_width="fill_parent"
        android:layout_height="wrap_content"
        android:layout_below="@id/create_account_form"
        android:gravity="center"
        android:paddingRight="45dp"
        android:text="Create Account"
        android:textSize="12sp"/>

</RelativeLayout>
```

◁──┐ **This button will
be only visible in
last page; it will be
in charge of
submitting form.**

As you can see, we placed a LinearLayout as a placeholder to every field. You'll see later how to populate it from the Gallery's Adapter code.

Now that we have the XML for the generic view, we should create the Adapter's code. We'll call our AdapterCreateAccountAdapter and extend from BaseAdapter. Because the Adapter's code is quite long, we'll discuss only the important methods. The first thing to write is the interface we'll use to communicate with the Activity. Use the following:

```
public static interface CreateAccountDelegate {
    int FORWARD = 1;
    int BACKWARD = -1;

    void scroll(int type);

    void processForm(Account account);
}
```

We'll use the scroll() method when the user presses the next button and the processForm() method when the user submits the form. We'll need to call the delegate when these buttons are pressed, so we'll want to set the click listeners in the getView() method, which is shown here:

```
public View getView(int position, View convertView, ViewGroup parent) {

    convertView = mInflator.inflate(
        R.layout.create_account_generic_row, parent, false);

    LinearLayout formLayout = (LinearLayout) convertView
        .findViewById(R.id.create_account_form);

    View nextButton = convertView
        .findViewById(R.id.create_account_next);
    if (position == FORMS_QTY - 1) {
      nextButton.setVisibility(View.GONE);
    } else {
      nextButton.setVisibility(View.VISIBLE);
    }

    if (mDelegate != null) {
      nextButton.setOnClickListener(new OnClickListener() {

        @Override
        public void onClick(View v) {
```

◁── **Inflate
custom
view.**

◁── **Get
LinearLayout
where we'll
place all form
widgets.**

◁──┐ **Next button
should be visible
in every page
but last one.**

```
            mDelegate.scroll(CreateAccountDelegate.FORWARD);
        }
    });
}

Button createButton = (Button) convertView
    .findViewById(R.id.create_account_create);
if (position == FORMS_QTY - 1) {
    createButton.setOnClickListener(new OnClickListener() {

        @Override
        public void onClick(View v) {
            processForm();
        }
    });

    createButton.setVisibility(View.VISIBLE);
} else {
    createButton.setVisibility(View.GONE);
}

switch (position) {
case 0:
    populateFirstForm(formLayout);
    break;
...

}

return convertView;
}
```

Create button should be visible only in last page.

In last step, switch over the position and populate LinearLayout accordingly.

The code inside the populateFirstForm() is the creation of fields and titles, which will end inside the LinearLayout. In the sample code, I decided to do everything by code, but we could easily create the views by inflating XMLs.

The missing piece of the puzzle is the one in charge of implementing the Create-AccountDelegate. In this case, it will be our CreateAccountActivity.

CreateAccountActivity will track the page that the user is in and it will be in charge of the page turn logic. The code is the following:

```
public class CreateAccountActivity extends Activity implements
    CreateAccountDelegate {

  private Gallery mGallery;
  private CreateAccountAdapter mAdapter;
  private int mGalleryPosition;

  @Override
  protected void onCreate(Bundle savedInstanceState) {
    super.onCreate(savedInstanceState);

    setContentView(R.layout.create_account);
    mGallery = (Gallery) findViewById(R.id.create_account_gallery);

    mAdapter = new CreateAccountAdapter(this);
    mGallery.setAdapter(mAdapter);
    mGalleryPosition = 0;
  }
```

Inside onCreate() method, create Adapter and set it to the Gallery.

```
@Override
protected void onResume() {
  super.onResume();
  mAdapter.setDelegate(this);
}

@Override
protected void onPause() {
  super.onPause();
  mAdapter.setDelegate(null);
}

@Override
public void onBackPressed() {

  if (mGalleryPosition > 0) {
    scroll(BACKWARD);
  } else {
    super.onBackPressed();
  }
}

@Override
public void scroll(int type) {

  switch (type) {
  case FORWARD:
    if (mGalleryPosition < mGallery.getCount() - 1) {
      mGallery.onKeyDown(KeyEvent.KEYCODE_DPAD_RIGHT,
          new KeyEvent(0, 0));
      mGalleryPosition++;
    }
    break;

  ...

  }

  ...

}
```

> Set Activity as Adapter's delegate in onResume() method and set it to null when onPause() is called.

> Override Activity's onBackPressed() method so there's a way to go back to a previous page.

> Inside scroll() method, Activity moves Gallery to next or previous page depending on the parameter.

Unfortunately, we can't animate the page turn in Android's Gallery widget. The only way I found is to send a KeyEvent.KEYCODE_DPAD_RIGHT event. It's hacky but it works.

The remaining code of the CreateAccountActivity takes care of validations and error handling. It contains nothing out of the ordinary, so I'll leave it for you to read from the sample code.

17.1 *The bottom line*

Using the Gallery widget to create wizard forms makes it easy for the user to fill out a long form. Having different pages and using the Gallery's default animation adds nice eye candy to make the process of filling the form less frustrating.

Depending on your needs, you can also try doing the same thing with the View-Pager class. Your Adapter would return Fragments instead of views.

17.2 *External links*

http://developer.android.com/reference/android/widget/Gallery.html

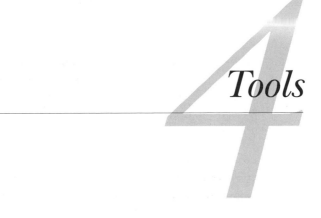

Tools

In this chapter, we'll look at two interesting tools you can use to create an Android application.

Hack 18 *Removing log statements before releasing*
Android v1.6+

If your application is making requests to a server, you might be using some type of log to check whether or not your requests are successful. Unfortunately, those logs don't get removed when you build the final APK (Android application package file). Removing logs is important to keep the logcat output as clean as possible. Leaving log statements in could also expose you to unintentional disclosure of sensitive information. In this hack, I'll show you how easy it is to remove logs for your market release.

Developers have their own technique preferences for removing logs from the final release. Some prefer doing something like the following:

```
if (BuildConfig.DEBUG) LOG.d(TAG, "The log msg");
```

From my point of view, the best way to remove logs is to use the ProGuard tool. If you've never used ProGuard, let me introduce it with the following quote from the Android documentation (see section 18.2):

The ProGuard tool shrinks, optimizes, and obfuscates your code by removing unused code and renaming classes, fields, and methods with semantically obscure names. The result is a smaller sized .apk file that is more difficult to reverse engineer.

If you haven't noticed yet, when we build an Android application we'll find a pro-guard.cfg file in our project root directory. Its presence there doesn't mean it's on by default; we need to enable it. Fortunately, it's simple: we need to add the following line in the default.properties file located in our project root directory:

```
proguard.config=proguard.cfg
```

Now ProGuard is enabled, but it'll only be used when exporting a signed APK. We need to add the necessary lines to the proguard.cfg to get rid of those logs. Append the following lines to proguard.cfg:

```
-assumenosideeffects class android.util.Log {
    public static *** d(...);
}
```

What we're telling ProGuard is this: remove every use of a d() method with any amount of parameters that returns something and belongs to the android.util.Log class. This will match with Log's d() method and every debug log will be removed.

18.1 *The bottom line*

The ProGuard tool offers another way of polishing a release. Make sure you read the ProGuard manual and create a correct configuration for your project because Pro-Guard might remove essential code, thinking it's not necessary for the application to work. If this happens, be sure to check that you're telling ProGuard to keep everything you need.

Notice that ProGuard isn't only used to remove log statements. As I'm testing, I usually create methods in my Activity to populate forms. These methods are also something I use ProGuard to remove.

18.2 *External links*

http://proguard.sourceforge.net/
http://developer.android.com/tools/help/proguard.html
http://mng.bz/ZR3t

Hack 19 *Using the Hierarchy Viewer tool to remove unnecessary views*
Android v1.6+

The Android SDK comes with a lot of tools; one of them is the Hierarchy Viewer. This tool lets you see the view tree and analyze how long it took to measure, lay out, and draw the views in your view. With the information this tool provides, you'll be able to detect unneeded views in the tree and bottlenecks. In this hack, we'll look at how to find these issues and solve them.

> **NOTE** I won't explain how to use the Hierarchy Viewer itself, so you might want to read Android's documentation at http://mng.bz/7ZXl for more information before proceeding.

For this hack, I've created a toy application with slow views that we'll try to fix using the Hierarchy Viewer. The application has a unique `Activity`, which you can see in figure 19.1, and it has the following XML:

Figure 19.1   Subject application

```xml
<?xml version="1.0" encoding="utf-8"?>
<RelativeLayout
    xmlns:android="http://schemas.android.com/apk/res/android"
    android:layout_width="fill_parent"
    android:layout_height="fill_parent">

    <TextView
        android:layout_width="fill_parent"
        android:layout_height="wrap_content"
        android:layout_alignParentTop="true"
        android:text="@string/hello"/>

    <RelativeLayout
        android:id="@+id/slow_container"
        android:layout_width="fill_parent"
        android:layout_height="wrap_content"
        android:layout_alignParentBottom="true">

        <com.test.SlowDrawView
            android:id="@+id/slow_draw"
            android:layout_width="fill_parent"
            android:layout_height="30dp"
            android:layout_alignParentTop="true"
            android:background="#FF0000"
            android:text="Slow Draw"/>
```

```
<com.test.SlowLayoutView
    android:id="@+id/slow_layout"
    android:layout_width="fill_parent"
    android:layout_height="30dp"
    android:layout_below="@id/slow_draw"
    android:background="#00FF00"
    android:text="Slow Layout"/>

<com.test.SlowMeasureView
    android:id="@+id/slow_measure"
    android:layout_width="fill_parent"
    android:layout_height="30dp"
    android:layout_below="@id/slow_layout"
    android:background="#0000FF"
    android:text="Slow Measure"/>
    </RelativeLayout>
</RelativeLayout>
```

This application is the default one, with some minor modifications. I've added three custom views in the button and removed the title bar. Let's load the Hierarchy Viewer with this application. You can see the results in figure 19.2.

> **NOTE**   For now, forget the definitions for the `PhoneWindow$DecorView` and the `FrameLayout`. Let's say they're nodes placed by the framework and unmodifiable. We talked about them in hack 15.

The first things to look for are `ViewGroups` inside `ViewGroups`. In this case, we have a `TextView` that has the `android:layout_alignParentTop` attribute and a second `RelativeLayout` holding all of the custom views, with `android:layout_align-ParentBottom`. You can also see that the second `RelativeLayout` has its three

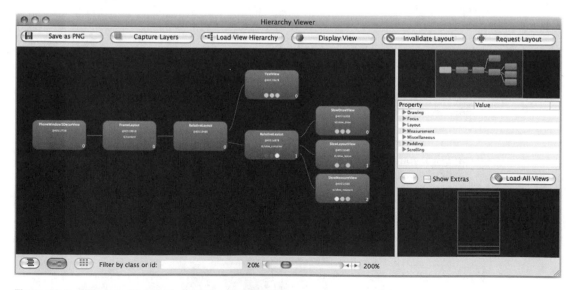

Figure 19.2   Hierarchy Viewer showing the application

performance indicators in red. This means that it's the slowest view in the tree. Let's try removing it by changing the other view's attributes. The modified XML looks like the following:

```xml
<?xml version="1.0" encoding="utf-8"?>
<RelativeLayout
    xmlns:android="http://schemas.android.com/apk/res/android"
    android:layout_width="fill_parent"
    android:layout_height="fill_parent">

    <TextView
        android:layout_width="fill_parent"
        android:layout_height="wrap_content"
        android:layout_alignParentTop="true"
        android:text="@string/hello"/>

    <com.test.SlowMeasureView
        android:id="@+id/slow_measure"
        android:layout_width="fill_parent"
        android:layout_height="30dp"
        android:layout_alignParentBottom="true"
        android:background="#0000FF"
        android:text="Slow Measure"/>

    <com.test.SlowLayoutView
        android:id="@+id/slow_layout"
        android:layout_width="fill_parent"
        android:layout_height="30dp"
        android:layout_above="@id/slow_measure"
        android:background="#00FF00"
        android:text="Slow Layout"/>

    <com.test.SlowDrawView
        android:id="@+id/slow_draw"
        android:layout_width="fill_parent"
        android:layout_height="30dp"
        android:layout_above="@id/slow_layout"
        android:background="#FF0000"
        android:text="Slow Draw"/>

</RelativeLayout>
```

The last fix reduced the view tree height by one. When creating views, it's always better to avoid tall view trees. Android draws the layout in a two-pass process: a measure pass and a layout pass. If you have a lot of nodes, it'll take longer to do the tree traversal.

After you've modified the XML to generate the shallowest tree, start looking at the performance indicators. Note that this indicator is relative to other view objects in the tree, so don't be fooled by this. Most of the nodes might be green, but that doesn't mean they're OK. Check how long it takes for them to draw and make sure everything is working well.

19.1 *The bottom line*

The Hierarchy Viewer is a great tool to see your view tree. As you're developing your application, try to keep track of how your view trees evolve to make sure your layouts are as responsive as they should be and that you're using the shallowest tree possible.

19.2 *External links*

http://developer.android.com/guide/developing/debugging/debugging-ui.html

5

Patterns

In this chapter, you'll read about different development patterns you can use inside Android.

Hack 20 *The Model-View-Presenter pattern*
Android v1.6+

You've most likely heard of the MVC (Model-View-Controller) pattern, and you've probably used it in different frameworks. When I was trying to find a better way to test my Android code, I learned about the *MVP (Model-View-Presenter)* pattern. The basic difference between MVP and MVC is that in MVP, the presenter contains the UI business logic for the view and communicates with it through an interface.

In this hack, I'll show you how to use MVP inside Android and how it improves the testability of the code. To see how it works, we'll build a splash screen. A splash screen is a common place to put initialization code and verifications, before the application starts running. In this case, inside the splash screen we'll provide a progress bar while we're checking whether or not we have internet access. If we do, we continue to another activity, but if we don't, we'll show the user an error message to prevent them from moving forward.

To create the splash screen, we'll have a presenter that will take care of the communication between the model and the view. In this particular case, the presenter

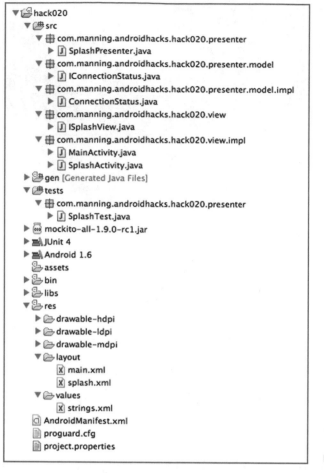

Figure 20.1   MVP project structure

will have two functions: one that knows when we're online and another to take care of controlling the view. You can see the project structure in figure 20.1.

The presenter will use a model class called ConnectionStatus that will implement the IConnectionStatus interface. This interface will answer whether we have internet access with a single method:

```
public interface IConnectionStatus {
  boolean isOnline();
}
```

As you might be thinking, the code in charge of controlling the view will be an Activity that implements the ISplashView interface. The interface will be used by thc presenter to control the flow of the application. Let's look at the code for the ISplashView interface:

```
public interface ISplashView {
  void showProgress();
  void hideProgress();
```

```
    void showNoInetErrorMsg();
    void moveToMainView();
}
```

Because we're coding in Android, the view will be the first to be created and afterward we'll give the control to the presenter. Let's see how we do that:

```
public class SplashActivity extends Activity implements ISplashView {
    private SplashPresenter mPresenter;

    @Override
    public void onCreate(Bundle savedInstanceState) {
        ...

        mPresenter = new SplashPresenter();
        mPresenter.setView(this);
    }

    @Override
    protected void onResume() {
        super.onResume();
        mPresenter.didFinishLoading();
    }
}
```

❶ Activity initialization code

❷ Instantiate presenter for this Activity

❸ Start presenter code when we reach onResume() method

We'll first need to initialize the Activity ❶. Afterward, we create the presenter ❷ that will take care of getting everything done and we set the Activity instance to the presenter. We can override the onResume() method ❸ to let the presenter know the view is ready to give control to it.

The presenter code is simple. Following is the presenter's didFinishLoading() method:

```
public void didFinishLoading() {
    ISplashView view = getView();

    if (mConnectionStatus.isOnline()) {
        view.moveToMainView();
    } else {
        view.hideProgress();
        view.showNoInetErrorMsg();
    }
}
```

❶ Getting view, in this case the Activity

❷ Logic to decide if we can move on

We'll get a reference to the ISplashView implementation using a presenter's getter ❶. We'll use the model's IConnectionStatus implementation to verify whether we're online ❷. Depending on that, we'll do different things with the view. As you can see, the view is used through an interface without knowing it's implemented by an Android Activity. This will end up in a view that's easy to mock in a unit test.

20.1 The bottom line

Using the MVP pattern will make your code more organized and easier to test. In the sample code, you'll notice a test folder. The test needs to instantiate the presenter and mock the interfaces. Because you're not using any Android-specific code in the presenter, you don't need to run in an Android-powered device and instead can run it in the JVM. In this case, you've used Mockito to mock the interfaces.

Because you've been working with Android, you'll notice that a lot of code ends up in the `Activity`. Unfortunately, testing activities is painful. Using the MVP pattern will help you create tests and apply TDD (test-driven development) in an easy way.

20.2   External links

http://en.wikipedia.org/wiki/Model_View_Presenter

Hack 21 *BroadcastReceiver following Activity's lifecycle*
Android v1.6+

Android uses different kinds of messages to notify applications when something happens. For example, if you want to know whether or not a device has connected to the internet, you have to listen to an `Intent` whose action is `android.net.conn` `.CONNECTIVITY_CHANGE`. This `Intent` can be heard using a `BroadcastReceiver`.

Although using a `BroadcastReceiver` to listen to different notifications from the OS works well, you can't access an `Activity` from the receiver.

Imagine trying to update the UI depending on the connectivity status. How would you do it? What would you do if you wanted to get the receiver's information inside one of your activities? In this hack, I'll show you how to use a `BroadcastReceiver` as an `Activity`'s inner class to get broadcast `Intents`.

Setting up a `BroadcastReceiver` as an `Activity`'s inner class lets us do two important things:

- Call the `Activity`'s methods from inside the receiver
- Enable and disable the receiver depending on the `Activity`'s status

For this hack, we'll create a `Service` that, when activated, waits for 5 seconds and then broadcasts a message. For this toy application, the message we'll send is a string with a date. The implementation of the service isn't that important, but you should know that it'll broadcast an `Intent` with an action—`com.manning.androidhacks` `.hack021.SERVICE_MSG`—and the date travels as an extra.

Because we want to use the date information the `service` sends in order to update the UI, we'll want to listen to this message only when the `Activity`'s screen is shown. Let's see how to achieve that using the following code:

```
public class MainActivity extends Activity {
  private ProgressDialog mProgressDialog;
  private TextView mTextView;
```

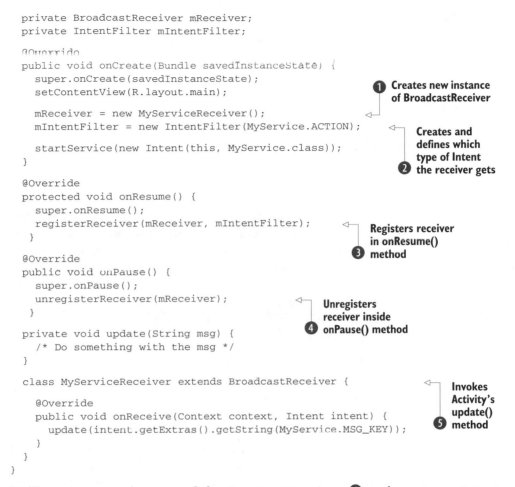

```
  private BroadcastReceiver mReceiver;
  private IntentFilter mIntentFilter;

  @Override
  public void onCreate(Bundle savedInstanceState) {
    super.onCreate(savedInstanceState);
    setContentView(R.layout.main);

    mReceiver = new MyServiceReceiver();
    mIntentFilter = new IntentFilter(MyService.ACTION);

    startService(new Intent(this, MyService.class));
  }

  @Override
  protected void onResume() {
    super.onResume();
    registerReceiver(mReceiver, mIntentFilter);
  }

  @Override
  public void onPause() {
    super.onPause();
    unregisterReceiver(mReceiver);
  }

  private void update(String msg) {
    /* Do something with the msg */
  }

  class MyServiceReceiver extends BroadcastReceiver {

    @Override
    public void onReceive(Context context, Intent intent) {
      update(intent.getExtras().getString(MyService.MSG_KEY));
    }
  }
}
```

1 Creates new instance of BroadcastReceiver

2 Creates and defines which type of Intent the receiver gets

3 Registers receiver in onResume() method

4 Unregisters receiver inside onPause() method

5 Invokes Activity's update() method

We'll create a new instance of the BroadcastReceiver **1** and create an Intent-Filter **2** that we'll use to define which type of Intent the receiver should get. Because the receiver is only used inside the Activity, we'll need to register it in the onResume() method **3** and unregister it inside the onPause() method **4**. When the receiver is called **5**, it'll invoke the Activity's update() method with the Intent's extra information as a parameter.

That's it—we now have a receiver that only updates the UI when the Activity is shown.

21.1   *The bottom line*

The whole Android ecosystem uses Intents to communicate. You'll need to use them sooner or later. By placing a receiver as an inner class in your Activity, you can give visual feedback using the information inside an Intent. Unregistering the receiver is a good way to avoid unnecessary calls to modify the UI when it's not needed.

21.2 External links

http://developer.android.com/reference/android/content/Intent.html

http://developer.android.com/reference/android/content/BroadcastReceiver.html

Hack 22 *Architecture pattern using Android libraries*
Android v1.6+

Before Android library projects were released, sharing code between Android projects was hard or even impossible. You could use a JAR to share Java code, but you couldn't share code that needed resources. Sharing an `Activity` or a custom view was impossible because you can't add resources to JARs and use them later in an Android application. Android library projects were created as a way to share Android code. In this hack, we'll look at a way to use them.

As an example, we'll create a small application with a login screen. The application is divided into three layers:

- Back-end logic and model (JAR file)
- Android library
- Android application

22.1 Back-end logic and model

This layer is a simple JAR file that can hold logic and doesn't involve or use Android-specific code. It's here that we place the server calls and business objects and logic. In our example, we'll have a project that creates a JAR file to handle login-specific functionality.

As you can see in figure 22.1, `Login` doesn't need to have Android as a dependency. The output of this project will be a JAR file to be included in our Android application. Having the business logic in a Java project means we can test everything with JUnit without setting up an Android test, which is painful. Also, separating code allows developers with different skills to work on the appropriate layer.

▼ 🗂 hack022-Login
  ▼ 📁 src
    ▼ ⊞ com.manning.androidhacks.hack022.login
      ▶ 🗋 Login.java
  ▼ 📁 test
    ▼ ⊞ com.manning.androidhacks.hack022.login
      ▶ 🗋 LoginTest.java
  ▶ ≡ JRE System Library [J2SE-1.5]
  ▶ ≡ JUnit 4

Figure 22.1   Login project loaded in Eclipse

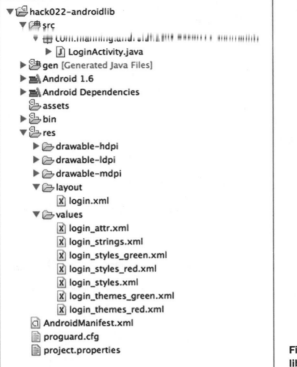

Figure 22.2 The Android library loaded in Eclipse

22.2 Android library

As I mentioned earlier, an Android library is like a JAR file but with the possibility of using Android resources. When we add an Android library as a dependency of our application, we get a second R class with the library's IDs and we'll be able to use the library's resources from our code. This layer will have Android-specific activities, a custom view, or services that Android applications will be able to reuse.

In figure 22.2, you can see the Android library `androidlib`. Here you can see Android as a dependency, which means that you can use every Android class and resource. Every Android library will have its own R class.

Note that this library can use the JAR mentioned earlier as a dependency. In this example, we placed the JAR as a dependency for the Android library. This way, we have a modular and maintainable library to use in any Android project.

22.3 Android application

The resulting Android application depends on the back-end JAR to handle business logic and the Android library to handle Android-related stuff. You can see in figure 22.3 how the Android library is included in the project.

In this layer, we'll be able to use code from the JAR and from the Android library. We now can start developing our application, taking care of the distribution of code between layers.

22.4   *The bottom line*

This was a short introduction to a possible architecture design using Android libraries. Reusable code and maintainability is hard to achieve, but now that you have Android libraries, it's possible.

Figure 22.3   Android application folder structure

22.5   *External links*

http://developer.android.com/tools/projects/index.html#LibraryProjects

http://developer.android.com/tools/projects/
projects-eclipse.html#SettingUpLibraryProject

Hack 23   The SyncAdapter pattern
Android v2.2+

Almost every Android application uses the internet to fetch information or to sync data. If you've already created a couple of applications, you'll be able to describe many different ways to create a connection and show a progress animation while fetching results.

23.1   *Common approaches*

I've been working as a contractor for different companies, and in my experiences I've seen developers handle data fetching in a variety of ways. Most of the code I've seen falls into one of the approaches that I'll cover next.

23.1.1   *Using the AsyncTask class*

AsyncTask is an Android class that handles threads for you, making it easy to move logic to another thread. If you've used it in previous projects, the following story might ring a bell.

Some time ago, you started developing for Android. You learned that you shouldn't place background logic in the main thread. You searched the web for an explanation of how to do it and you found a nice Android developer's article entitled "Painless Threading." Near the end of the article (see section 23.4), it states this:

> Always remember these two rules about the single thread model.
> Do not block the UI thread, and make sure that you access the
> Android UI toolkit only on the UI thread.

`AsyncTask` just makes it easier to do both of these things.

So you learned how to use the `AsyncTask` class and you started using it everywhere. No matter how complex your UI was, or how long it took to parse those big chunks of data, the `AsyncTask` was always there for you. You left work early pointing and laughing at the iOS developers from your company, saying "Android is easier than iOS; I finished earlier than you. Enjoy your night coding, Apple fan boys!"

Unfortunately, this didn't last long. You noticed that if you rotated the device while an `AsyncTask` was running, your application crashed. It was hard to fix, but an ugly hack did the trick. Later you noticed that your application also crashed after some time due to a limitation in the amount of concurrent tasks the `AsyncTask` supported. When you tried to fix this second issue, you noticed that your `Activity`'s code was polluted with a lot of inner classes extending `AsyncTask`. After a long day, you started questioning where you went wrong.

If you're planning to use an `AsyncTask`, think it over. The only reason to use it is when the background task is simple or you don't depend on the result. Let's look at another approach.

23.1.2 *Using a Service*

The second approach is to use a `Service`. Using a `Service` solves a lot of issues but comes with some difficulties. Following is a list of concerns that always caused me to wonder whether or not I was making the correct choice:

- Communicating with an `Activity`
- Deciding when and how to start the `Service`
- Detecting connectivity status while working
- Persisting data

The issue with this approach is the system's flexibility. For example, you have many ways to communicate with an `Activity`. Should the `Activity` bind to the `Service`? Should it use a `Handler`? Should it communicate via `Intents`? Should it communicate through a database? Many possibilities exist and the answer to the question of which you should use is always "it depends."

The question I started asking myself was, how does the Gmail application work? How does it sync and work offline without an issue? Google uses something called `SyncAdapter`. Unfortunately, this is one of Android's best but least documented features. If you ask Android developers if they know what it is, they'll say yes, but they've never used it.

In this hack, we'll see how to use a `SyncAdapter` to organize an internet-dependent application, making our development life easier.

23.2   *What we'll create*

For this example, we'll create a TODO list. We'll use a server that will have a front end to add items from the browser. You can see how it looks in figure 23.1. The server will also have an API so we can have the same functionality in an Android device. The running Android application can be seen in figure 23.2.

23.2.1   *What's a SyncAdapter?*

A `SyncAdapter` is an Android `Service` that's started by the platform. There we'll place all of our sync logic. Before you get lost, go watch Virgil Dobjanschi's Google I/O 2010 Android REST (see section 23.4)client application presentation. This is without a doubt the best Google I/O presentation ever and the only good documentation on `SyncAdapters`.

The benefits of using `SyncAdapters` include

- Automatically syncs in the background (even when our application isn't open)
- Handles authentication against the server
- Handles retries
- Respects user's preferences regarding background syncs

Figure 23.1   Server's front end
Figure 23.2   Android application's front end

23.2.2 *Hitting a database instead of the server*

The first thing to do is to forget about syncing. We'll create the application to only work locally and save information inside a database. To do this, we'll need a `DatabaseHelper`, a `TodoContentProvider`, and a `TodoDAO`. Let's first understand the `DatabaseHelper`:

```
public class DatabaseHelper extends SQLiteOpenHelper {        ◁━━  Extends
  public static final String DATABASE_NAME = "todo.db";        ❶ SQLiteOpenHelper
  private static final int DATABASE_VERSION = 1;

  public DatabaseHelper(Context context) {
    super(context, DATABASE_NAME, null, DATABASE_VERSION);    ◁━━  Specifies
  }                                                                database
                                                                   name and
  @Override                                                     ❷ version
  public void onCreate(SQLiteDatabase db) {
    db.execSQL("CREATE TABLE "
      + TodoContentProvider.TODO_TABLE_NAME + " ("
      + TodoContentProvider.COLUMN_ID
      + " INTEGER PRIMARY KEY AUTOINCREMENT,"
      + TodoContentProvider.COLUMN_SERVER_ID + " INTEGER,"
      + TodoContentProvider.COLUMN_TITLE + " LONGTEXT,"
      + TodoContentProvider.COLUMN_STATUS_FLAG + " INTEGER"
      + ");");
  }

  @Override
  public void onUpgrade(SQLiteDatabase db, int oldVersion,
      int newVersion) {                                        ◁━━  Upgrades
    db.execSQL("DROP TABLE IF EXISTS " +                            from an old
      TodoContentProvider.TODO_TABLE_NAME);                    ❹ schema
    onCreate(db);
  }
}
```

Decides if tables need to be created ❸

The `DatabaseHelper` extends `SQLiteOpenHelper` ❶. When the class is created, we specify the database name and its version ❷. The `SQLiteOpenHelper` will use that to decide whether some tables need to be created ❸ or upgraded from an old schema ❹. Don't worry about the schema for now. You'll understand all its rows in short order.

Now that we have the `DatabaseHelper` in place, we'll need to set up our `Content-Provider`. Note that if you've never used a `ContentProvider`, you should try doing a fast web search before you continue reading. The `TodoContentProvider` class for this hack has nothing out of the ordinary. Let's look at how the `query` method is created:

```
public class TodoContentProvider extends ContentProvider {       ◁━━
  public static final String TODO_TABLE_NAME = "todos";           ❶
  public static final String AUTHORITY = TodoContentProvider.class
    .getCanonicalName();                                         Extends
                                                                 ContentProvider
  public static final String COLUMN_ID = "_id";
  public static final String COLUMN_SERVER_ID = "server_id";
  public static final String COLUMN_TITLE = "title";
  public static final String COLUMN_STATUS_FLAG = "status_flag";

  private static final int TODO = 1;
```

```
private static final int TODO_ID = 2;

private static HashMap<String, String> projectionMap;
private static final UriMatcher sUriMatcher;

public static final String CONTENT_TYPE =
  "vnd.android.cursor.dir/vnd.androidhacks.todo";
public static final String CONTENT_TYPE_ID =
  "vnd.android.cursor.item/vnd.androidhacks.todo";

public static final Uri CONTENT_URI = Uri.parse("content://"
    + AUTHORITY + "/" + TODO_TABLE_NAME);

private DatabaseHelper dbHelper;

static {
  sUriMatcher = new UriMatcher(UriMatcher.NO_MATCH);
  sUriMatcher.addURI(AUTHORITY, TODO_TABLE_NAME, TODO);
  sUriMatcher.addURI(AUTHORITY, TODO_TABLE_NAME + "/#", TODO_ID);

  projectionMap = new HashMap<String, String>();
  projectionMap.put(COLUMN_ID, COLUMN_ID);
  projectionMap.put(COLUMN_SERVER_ID, COLUMN_SERVER_ID);
  projectionMap.put(COLUMN_TITLE, COLUMN_TITLE);
  projectionMap.put(COLUMN_STATUS_FLAG, COLUMN_STATUS_FLAG);
}

@Override
public boolean onCreate() {
  dbHelper = new DatabaseHelper(getContext());
  return true;
}

@Override
public Cursor query(Uri uri, String[] projection, String selection,
    String[] selectionArgs, String sortOrder) {

  SQLiteQueryBuilder qb = new SQLiteQueryBuilder();
  switch (sUriMatcher.match(uri)) {
  case TODO:
    qb.setTables(TODO_TABLE_NAME);
    qb.setProjectionMap(projectionMap);
    break;
  case TODO_ID:
    qb.setTables(TODO_TABLE_NAME);
    qb.setProjectionMap(projectionMap);
    qb.appendWhere(COLUMN_ID + "=" + uri.getPathSegments().get(1));
    break;
  default:
    throw new RuntimeException("Unknown URI");
  }

  SQLiteDatabase db = dbHelper.getReadableDatabase();
  Cursor c = qb.query(db, projection, selection,
    selectionArgs, null, null, sortOrder);

  c.setNotificationUri(getContext().getContentResolver(),
    uri);
```

2 Decides which action to take for an incoming content URI

3 Changes match

4 Creates ContentProvider

5 Switches over a URI and sets query builder

6 Gets a Cursor from the database

7 Sets notification URI; Cursor watches for URI content changes

```
    return c;
  }
...
}
```

The `TodoContentProvider` extends `ContentProvider` ❶. Inside it we define a `UriMatcher` that will help us decide which action to take for an incoming content URI ❷. In this case, the content values to use with the `ContentProvider` have a one-to-one match with the database columns. If we want to change that, we can use a projection map ❸. When the `ContentProvider` is created ❹, we get an instance of the `DatabaseHelper`, which will be useful for querying the database. For the sake of brevity I only show the `query()` method. The rest of the `ContentProvider` methods look alike. Inside the `query()` method, we can see how to switch over a URI and set the query builder correctly ❺. After that we use the query builder to get a `Cursor` from the database that will be returned to the user ❻. Pay attention to the last line ❼. Before returning the `Cursor`, we set the notification URI. This will make the `Cursor` watch for URI content changes. This means that every time something gets modified, the `Cursor` will update automagically.

Finally, the `TodoDAO` will be in charge of calling the `ContentProvider` through a `ContentResolver`. This is the layer where conversions from Java objects to database values and from database values to Java objects occur, as follows:

```
public class TodoDAO {
  private static final TodoDAO instance = new TodoDAO();

  private TodoDAO() {}

  public static TodoDAO getInstance() {          ❶ Implements
    return instance;                                singleton
  }

  public void addNewTodo(ContentResolver contentResolver,   ❷ Places
    Todo list, int flag) {                                    calls
    ContentValues contentValue = getTodoContentValues(list, flag);
    contentResolver.insert(TodoContentProvider.CONTENT_URI,
      contentValue);
  }                                              ❸ Converts
                                                   to content
  private ContentValues getTodoContentValues(Todo todo,   values
    int flag) {
    ContentValues cv = new ContentValues();
    cv.put(TodoContentProvider.COLUMN_SERVER_ID, todo.getId());
    cv.put(TodoContentProvider.COLUMN_TITLE, todo.getTitle());
    cv.put(TodoContentProvider.COLUMN_STATUS_FLAG, flag);

    return cv;
  }
...
}
```

As you can see, the `TodoDAO` is implemented with a singleton ❶. There, we placed calls such as `addNewTodo()` ❷ which, after a proper conversion to content values ❸, will end in a database insert.

23.2.3 *Populating the database*

In this section, you'll see how to deal with the database from the application. We'll use two activities:

- `MainActivity`—Will show the list of TODOs
- `AddNewActivity`—Will present a form to add a new TODO

Both activities function in a similar way. When they need to modify some data, they'll do it through the `TodoDAO`. Let's take a look at the code for the `MainActivity`:

```
public class MainActivity extends Activity {

  private ListView mListView;
  private TodoAdapter mAdapter;

  @Override
  public void onCreate(Bundle savedInstanceState) {
    super.onCreate(savedInstanceState);
    setContentView(R.layout.main);
    mListView = (ListView) findViewById(R.id.main_activity_listview);

    mAdapter = new TodoAdapter(this);               ◁┐  Creates
    mListView.setAdapter(mAdapter);                 ❶  ListView
  }

  public void addNew(View v) {                          ❷  Starts
    startActivity(new Intent(this, AddNewActivity.class));  ◁  AddNewActivity
  }                                                        activity
}
```

Nothing out of the ordinary here. We created a `ListView` that will use a `TodoAdapter` ❶, and every time the user clicks on the Add New button, we'll start the `AddNew-Activity` activity ❷.

The `TodoAdapter` holds more interesting code. Let's see how it's done:

```
public class TodoAdapter extends CursorAdapter {

...

  private static final String[] PROJECTION_IDS_TITLE_AND_STATUS =
   new String[] {
      TodoContentProvider.COLUMN_ID,
      TodoContentProvider.COLUMN_TITLE,
      TodoContentProvider.COLUMN_STATUS_FLAG };

  public TodoAdapter(Activity activity) {
    super(activity, getManagedCursor(activity), true);
    mActivity - activity;
    ...
  }                                                    ❶  Gets a
                                                          Cursor
  private static Cursor getManagedCursor(Activity activity) {  ◁
    return activity.managedQuery(TodoContentProvider.CONTENT_URI,
```

```
        PROJECTION_IDS_TITLE_AND_STATUS,
        TodoContentProvider.COLUMN_STATUS_FLAG + " != "
            + StatusFlag.DELETE, null,
        TodoContent███████████████ ████ ███████) ;
}
```

◁ **Checks use of TodoContentProvider's** ❷ **URI and a projection**

```
@Override
public void bindView(View view, Context context, Cursor c) {
    final ViewHolder holder = (ViewHolder) view.getTag();
    holder.id.setText(c.getString(mInternalIdIndex));
    holder.title.setText(c.getString(mTitleIndex));

    final int status = c.getInt(mInternalStatusIndex);
    if (StatusFlag.CLEAN != status) {
        holder.title.setBackgroundColor(Color.RED);
    } else {
        holder.title.setBackgroundColor(Color.GREEN);
    }

    final Long id = Long.valueOf(holder.id.getText().toString());
    holder.deleteButton.setOnClickListener(new OnClickListener() {

        @Override
        public void onClick(View v) {
            TodoDAO.getInstance().deleteTodo(
                mActivity.getContentResolver(), id);
        }
    });
}

...
}
```

❸ **Changes background of text** ◁

◁ **Removes TODO from** ❹ **the list**

When the `TodoAdapter` is created, we get a `Cursor` ❶ using `Activity`'s managed-Query() method. Check how we used the `TodoContentProvider`'s URI and a projection ❷. Finally, we have the `bindView()` method. With it we change the background of the text depending on the status flag (I'll discuss that later) ❸ and set a click listener for the Delete button. Inside the listener, we use the `TodoDAO` to remove the TODO from the list ❹.

Where's the `notifyDataSetChanged()`? There's no need for it. Do you remember the `setNotificationUri()` call we used inside the `TodoContentProvider`? The `Cursor` returned by the `TodoContentProvider` will get updated when changes are made to the database through the `ContentProvider`.

Up to this point, we have a working application that saves data to a database. Now we need to take the authentication step and sync with the server.

23.2.4 Adding login functionality

Before adding the `SyncAdapter` to our code, let's first see how to deal with the authentication with the server. Instead of saving the login details inside a database or a shared preference, we'll save them in an Android `Account`. To handle accounts, we'll use an Android class called `AccountManager`. The `AccountManager` is in charge of managing user credentials inside `Accounts`. The basic idea is that users enter their credentials once, and they're saved inside an Account. All of the applications that have the USE_CREDENTIALS permission can query the manager to obtain an account where an authentication token or whatever is necessary to authenticate against a server is saved.

Before coding this part, you need to understand that the login functionality will be used in these situations:

- When the application starts and no account has been created
- When the user goes to Accounts & Sync and clicks on New Account
- When the SyncAdapter tries to sync and the authentication fails

Let's look at the first two situations in this section and the last one after we have the SyncAdapter working. For the first one, we'll create a BootstrapActivity:

```
public class BootstrapActivity extends Activity {
  private static final int NEW_ACCOUNT = 0;
  private static final int EXISTING_ACCOUNT = 1;
  private AccountManager mAccountManager;

  @Override
  protected void onCreate(Bundle savedInstanceState) {
    super.onCreate(savedInstanceState);
    setContentView(R.layout.bootstrap);

    mAccountManager = AccountManager.get(this);                    ❶ Gets list of
    Account[] accounts = mAccountManager                              accounts of
        .getAccountsByType(AuthenticatorActivity.PARAM_ACCOUNT_TYPE);  our type

    if (accounts.length == 0) {
      final Intent i = new Intent(this, AuthenticatorActivity.class);
      i.setFlags(Intent.FLAG_ACTIVITY_CLEAR_WHEN_TASK_RESET);
      startActivityForResult(i, NEW_ACCOUNT);
    } else {
      String password = mAccountManager.getPassword(accounts[0]);
      if (password == null) {
        final Intent i = new Intent(this, AuthenticatorActivity.class);
        i.putExtra(AuthenticatorActivity.PARAM_USER, accounts[0].name);
        startActivityForResult(i, EXISTING_ACCOUNT);
      } else {
        startActivity(new Intent(this, MainActivity.class));        ❹ Continues to
        finish();                                                      MainActivity
      }
    }
  }

  ...

}
```

Creates a new account ❷

Asks user for password ❸

Inside the onCreate() method, we get a list of accounts of our type ❶. If we have no account, we launch the AuthenticatorActivity to help create a new account ❷. If the account exists but the AccountManager doesn't have a password for it, we need to ask the user for the password ❸. This can happen when the password gets invalidated. The last case is when everything is in place, so we can continue to the MainActivity ❹.

The second situation is more complicated but will leave everything in place for the last situation. To create a new account through the Accounts & Sync settings, we'll need to extend AbstractAccountAuthenticator.

The AbstractAccountAuthenticator is a base class for creating account authenticators. In order to provide an authenticator, we must extend this class, provide implementations for the abstract methods, and write a service that returns the result of getIBinder() in the service's onBind(android.content.Intent) method when invoked with an Intent with action AccountManager.ACTION_AUTHENTICATOR_INTENT.

We'll extend the AbstractAccountAuthenticator with a class called Authenticator. It's OK to return null values from the methods we're not going to use. The important ones are addAcount() and getAuthToken(). The code follows:

```java
public class Authenticator extends AbstractAccountAuthenticator {
  private final Context mContext;

  public Authenticator(Context context) {
    super(context);
    mContext = context;
  }

  @Override
  public Bundle addAccount(AccountAuthenticatorResponse response,
      String accountType, String authTokenType,
      String[] requiredFeatures, Bundle options)
      throws NetworkErrorException {

    final Intent intent = new Intent(mContext,
        AuthenticatorActivity.class);
    intent.putExtra(AuthenticatorActivity.PARAM_AUTHTOKEN_TYPE,
        authTokenType);
    intent.putExtra(AccountManager.KEY_ACCOUNT_AUTHENTICATOR_RESPONSE,
        response);
    final Bundle bundle = new Bundle();
    bundle.putParcelable(AccountManager.KEY_INTENT, intent);

    return bundle;
  }

  ..

  @Override
  public Bundle getAuthToken(AccountAuthenticatorResponse response,
      Account account, String authTokenType, Bundle options)
      throws NetworkErrorException {

    if (!authTokenType
        .equals(AuthenticatorActivity.PARAM_AUTHTOKEN_TYPE)) {    ◁── ❶ Checks if required token is the same

      final Bundle result = new Bundle();
      result.putString(AccountManager.KEY_ERROR_MESSAGE,
          "invalid authTokenType");

      return result;
    }

    final AccountManager am = AccountManager.get(mContext);
    final String password = am.getPassword(account);
```

```
if (password != null) {                          ◁──┐  Gets a
  boolean verified = false;                        ❷ password
  String loginResponse = null;

  try {
    loginResponse = LoginServiceImpl.sendCredentials(
      account.name, password);
    verified = LoginServiceImpl.hasLoggedIn(loginResponse);
  } catch (AndroidHacksException e) {
    verified = false;
  }
                                            ❸ Returns
  if (verified) {                      ◁──┘   the result
    final Bundle result = new Bundle();
    result.putString(AccountManager.KEY_ACCOUNT_NAME, account.name);
    result.putString(AccountManager.KEY_ACCOUNT_TYPE,
        AuthenticatorActivity.PARAM_ACCOUNT_TYPE);

    return result;
  }
}                                          ❹ Lets caller know
                                      ◁──┐  which activity to call
final Intent intent = new Intent(mContext,  for user to sign in
    AuthenticatorActivity.class);
intent.putExtra(AuthenticatorActivity.PARAM_USER, account.name);
intent.putExtra(AuthenticatorActivity.PARAM_AUTHTOKEN_TYPE,
    authTokenType);
intent.putExtra(AccountManager.KEY_ACCOUNT_AUTHENTICATOR_RESPONSE,
    response);
final Bundle bundle = new Bundle();
bundle.putParcelable(AccountManager.KEY_INTENT, intent);
return bundle;
}
```

The addAccount() method is straightforward. There we prepare the Intent that the AccountManager will use to create a new account. Let's now investigate the getAuthToken() method. This method will be called when we need to log in to the server using the credentials inside the Account. We'll first check if the required token is the same as the one we handle ❶. Afterward, we use the AccountManager to get a password. If there's a password stored ❷, we sign in against the server, and if it's OK ❸, we return the result. If we can't sign in, we'll return an Intent to let the caller know which activity to call to let the user sign in ❹. This happens when the password changes or the credentials were revoked.

The next class to create is AuthenticatorActivity. This activity will be used to show the login form. You can see how it looks in figure 23.3.

Figure 23.3 Login form from AuthenticatorActivity

The code is the following:

```
public class AuthenticatorActivity extends
    AccountAuthenticatorActivity {
  public static final String PARAM_ACCOUNT_TYPE =
    "com.manning.androidhacks.hack023";
  public static final String PARAM_AUTHTOKEN_TYPE = "authtokenType";
  public static final String PARAM_USER = "user";
  public static final String PARAM_CONFIRMCREDENTIALS =
    "confirmCredentials";
  private AccountManager mAccountManager;
  private Thread mAuthThread;
  private String mAuthToken;
  private String mAuthTokenType;
  private Boolean mConfirmCredentials = false;
  private final Handler mHandler = new Handler();
  protected boolean mRequestNewAccount = false;
  private String mUser;

  ...

  private void handleLogin(View view) {
    if (mRequestNewAccount) {
      mUsername = mUsernameEdit.getText().toString();
    }
    mPassword = mPasswordEdit.getText().toString();

    if (TextUtils.isEmpty(mUsername) || TextUtils.isEmpty(mPassword)) {
      mMessage.setText(getMessage());
    }

    showProgress();
    mAuthThread = NetworkUtilities.attemptAuth(mUsername,
      mPassword, mHandler, AuthenticatorActivity.this);
  }

  public void onAuthenticationResult(Boolean result) {
    hideProgress();

    if (result) {
      if (!mConfirmCredentials) {
        finishLogin();
      }
    } else {
      mMessage.setText("User and/or password are incorrect");
    }
  }

  private void finishLogin() {
    final Account account = new Account(mUsername, PARAM_ACCOUNT_TYPE);

    if (mRequestNewAccount) {
      mAccountManager.addAccountExplicitly(account, mPassword, null);
    } else {
      mAccountManager.setPassword(account, mPassword);
    }

    final Intent intent = new Intent();
    intent.putExtra(AccountManager.KEY_ACCOUNT_NAME, mUsername);
```

1 Launches thread that will hit server

2 Returns result to AuthenticatiorActivity

3 Calls finishLogin()

4 Sets a new password

```
    intent.putExtra(AccountManager.KEY_ACCOUNT_TYPE,
      PARAM_ACCOUNT_TYPE);

    if (mAuthTokenType != null
        && mAuthTokenType.equals(PARAM_AUTHTOKEN_TYPE)) {
      intent.putExtra(AccountManager.KEY_AUTHTOKEN, mAuthToken);
    }

    setAccountAuthenticatorResult(intent.getExtras());      ◁─┐  Sets the
    setResult(RESULT_OK, intent);                            ❺  result
    finish();
  }

...

}
```

When the user enters the login details and clicks OK, handleLogin() gets executed. There we launch a thread that will hit the server ❶ and return the result to the AuthenticatorActivity in the onAuthenticationResult() method ❷. If the service can authenticate correctly, we'll call finishLogin() ❸, and if not we'll show an error and let the user try again. Inside finishLogin(), if the Request New Account flag is set, we use the AccountManager to create an account. If the account exists, we'll set a new password ❹. Finally, we set the result that's to be sent as the result of the request that caused this activity to be launched ❺.

The last step is modifying the AndroidManifest.xml to register the Service. We do that by adding the following:

```
<service android:name=".authenticator.AuthenticationService"
  android:exported="true">
                                                    ❶  Returns an
  <intent-filter>                               ◁─┘      Authenticator
    <action android:name="android.accounts.AccountAuthenticator" />
  </intent-filter>

  <meta-data android:name="android.accounts.AccountAuthenticator"
    android:resource="@xml/authenticator" />      ◁─┐
</service>                                         ❷  Additional information
```

The android.accounts.AccountAuthenticator Intent filter will make the system notice that this particular Service returns an Authenticator ❶. We'll also need to give additional information using a separate XML file ❷. In this example, the authenticator XML contains the following:

```
<account-authenticator
    xmlns:android="http://schemas.android.com/apk/res/android"
    android:accountType="com.manning.androidhacks.hack023"
    android:icon="@drawable/ic_launcher"
    android:smallIcon="@drawable/ic_launcher"
    android:label="@string/app name"/>
```

The most important piece of information is the android:accountType. That means that the Service will return an Authenticator to authenticate only accounts of type com.manning.androidhacks.hack023. The rest of the information we can place there determines how the Accounts & Sync row will look.

23.2.5 Adding the SyncAdapter

The last step is to add a SyncAdapter. After so many pages, we still don't know what it's for, so let's try to understand how the SyncAdapter will add a happy ending to everything we wrote so far.

The SyncAdapter is a Service handled by Android that will use an Account to authenticate to the server and a ContentProvider to sync data. When we finish coding it, the application will sync with the server without us telling it anything. The OS will register it with every other SyncAdapter inside the device. The SyncAdapters run one at a time to avoid making our internet connection choke. Isn't it the best Android feature you've used so far? Let's learn how to code it.

We first need to declare it in the AndroidManifest.xml:

```
<service android:name=".service.TodoSyncService"
    android:exported="true">
    <intent-filter>
        <action android:name="android.content.SyncAdapter" />
    </intent-filter>
    <meta-data android:name="android.content.SyncAdapter"
        android:resource="@xml/todo_sync_adapter" />
</service>
```

❶ Defines the android.content .SyncAdapter

❷ Additional XML

Similar to the AuthenticationService, we define the android.content.SyncAdapter action to let Android know that TodoSyncService is a SyncAdapter ❶. It also has some additional XML ❷ with the following information:

```
<sync-adapter xmlns:android="http://schemas.android.com/apk/res/android"
    android:contentAuthority=
    "com.manning.androidhacks.hack023.provider.TodoContentProvider"
    android:accountType=
    "com.manning.androidhacks.hack023" />
```

This means that the TodoSyncService will use the TodoContentProvider's authority and will need a com.manning.androidhacks.hack023 account type.

The next step is to extend AbstractThreadedSyncAdapter. Following is the code:

```
public class TodoSyncAdapter extends AbstractThreadedSyncAdapter {
    private final ContentResolver mContentResolver;
    private AccountManager mAccountManager;
    private final static TodoDAO mTodoDAO = TodoDAO.getInstance();

    @Override
    public void onPerformSync(Account account, Bundle extras,
        String authority, ContentProviderClient provider,
        SyncResult syncResult) {
        try {
            List<Todo> data = fetchData();
            syncRemoteDeleted(data);
```

Gets every TODO from the server ❶

Removes the TODOs from the local database ❷

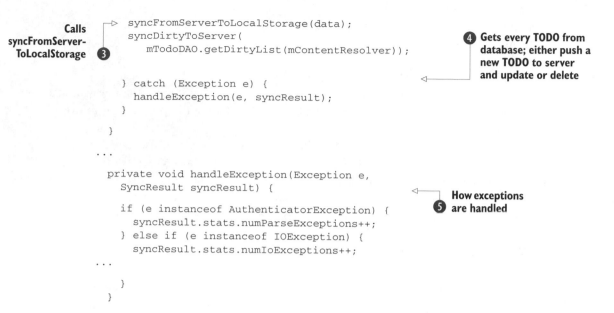

Calls
syncFromServer-
ToLocalStorage ❸

```
        syncFromServerToLocalStorage(data);
        syncDirtyToServer(
            mTodoDAO.getDirtyList(mContentResolver));

      } catch (Exception e) {
        handleException(e, syncResult);
      }
    }

  ...

    private void handleException(Exception e,
      SyncResult syncResult) {

      if (e instanceof AuthenticatorException) {
        syncResult.stats.numParseExceptions++;
      } else if (e instanceof IOException) {
        syncResult.stats.numIoExceptions++;
  ...

      }
    }
```

❹ **Gets every TODO from database; either push a new TODO to server and update or delete**

❺ **How exceptions are handled**

When the `onPerformSync()` method gets called, we're already in a background thread. Here's where we add the logic to sync with the server. In the next few lines, I'll explain a sync approach that works for me; it doesn't mean you're obliged to do it this way.

Do you remember what a row in the TODO table looked like? The TODO table has the following columns:

- *_id*—Local ID.
- *server_id*—After syncing, every row will get the server's ID.
- *status_flag*—The status can be CLEAN, MOD, ADD, DELETE.
- *title*—The text of the TODO.

When the sync starts, we first get every TODO from the server ❶. Note that if we have lots of TODOs, we might need to use some sort of pagination. The next step is removing from the local database TODOs that are no longer in the server ❷. We do this by getting a list of TODOs from our local database with the CLEAN flag set, and checking whether a TODO is in the server's list. If it's not there, we can delete it from our local database. After that, `syncFromServerToLocalStorage` is called ❸. There we'll iterate over the server's TODOs. We can use the server_id to check whether it exists locally. If it exists, we update it with the information from the server. If not, we create a new one. The last step is `syncDirtyToServer()` ❹. In this case, we get every TODO from the local database that's dirty (not *clean*). There, depending on the status flag, we push a new TODO to the server and update or delete.

Note how the exceptions are handled ❺. Depending on the exception, we modify the `syncResult` object. We do this to help the `SyncManager` decide when to call the `SyncAdapter` again.

The final step is to wrap the `SyncAdapter` inside the `TodoSyncService`, which we can do using the following code:

```
public class TodoSyncService extends Service {
    private static final Object sSyncAdapterLock = new Object();
    private static TodoSyncAdapter sSyncAdapter = null;

    @Override
    public void onCreate() {
        synchronized (sSyncAdapterLock) {
            if (sSyncAdapter == null) {
                sSyncAdapter = new TodoSyncAdapter(
                    getApplicationContext(), true);
            }
        }
    }

    @Override
    public IBinder onBind(Intent intent) {
        return sSyncAdapter.getSyncAdapterBinder();
    }
}
```

23.3 *The bottom line*

You might be thinking that using a `SyncAdapter` is a lot of work, but note how after creating the model and the `ContentProvider`, everything got easier. Users can use the application offline or online; they won't notice the difference.

Note that I didn't explain anything about the server. For this example, I've coded a small Python server using web.py. If you're giving `SyncAdapters` a try, I recommend you use something like StackMob. You'll avoid wasting time coding the back end.

23.4 *External links*

http://developer.android.com/reference/android/os/AsyncTask.html

http://www.youtube.com/watch?feature=player_embedded&v=xHXn3Kg2IQE

http://android-developers.blogspot.com.ar/2009/05/painless-threading.html

http://logc.at/2011/11/08/the-hidden-pitfalls-of-asynctask/

http://developer.android.com/reference/android/content/
AbstractThreadedSyncAdapter.html

http://www.youtube.com/watch?v=xHXn3Kg2IQE&feature=youtu.be

http://developer.android.com/guide/topics/providers/content-provider-creating.html

http://naked-code.blogspot.com/2011/05/revenge-of-syncadapter-synchronizing.html

http://developer.android.com/reference/android/content/
AbstractThreadedSyncAdapter.html

https://www.stackmob.com/

Working with lists and adapters

Lists and adapters are two of the main concepts to master in Android development. In this chapter, you'll learn several tips and tricks you can use with lists and adapters.

Hack 24 Handling empty lists
Android v1.6+

A common way to show data to the user in mobile platforms is to place it inside a list. When you do this, you need to handle two cases: the ordinary list full of items and an empty state. For the list, you'll use a `ListView`, but how do you handle the empty state? Fortunately, there's an easy way to achieve this. Let's look at how to do it.

`ListView` and other classes that extend `AdapterView` easily handle emptiness through a method called `setEmptyView(View)`. When the `AdapterView` needs to draw, it'll draw the empty view if its `Adapter` is null, or the adapter's `isEmpty()` method returns true.

Let's try an example. Imagine we want to create an application to handle our TODO list. Our main screen will be a `ListView` with all our TODO items, but when we launch it for the first time, it'll be empty. For our empty state, we'll draw a nice image. Following is the XML layout:

```xml
<?xml version="1.0" encoding="utf-8"?>
<FrameLayout xmlns:android="http://schemas.android.com/apk/res/android"
    android:layout_width="fill_parent"
    android:layout_height="fill_parent">

    <ListView android:id="@+id/list_view"
        android:layout_width="fill_parent"
        android:layout_height="fill_parent"/>

    <ImageView android:id="@+id/empty_view"
        android:layout_width="fill_parent"
        android:layout_height="fill_parent"
        android:src="@drawable/empty_view"/>

</FrameLayout>
```

The only thing missing is the onCreate() code, where we fetch the ListView and place the ImageView as the empty view. The code to use is the following:

```java
@Override
public void onCreate(Bundle savedInstanceState) {
  super.onCreate(savedInstanceState);
  setContentView(R.layout.main);

  ListView mListView = (ListView) findViewById(R.id.list_view);
  mListView.setEmptyView(findViewById(R.id.empty_view));
}
```

Because we're not setting an adapter to the ListView when we run this code, it'll show the ImageView.

24.1 The bottom line

I must admit that I was late to learn about this trick. I kept hiding my ListViews when the adapter was empty. When you use the setEmpty(View) method, your code will be more compact and easier to read.

You can also try using a ViewStub as an empty view. Using a ViewStub as an empty view will guarantee that the empty view isn't inflated when it's not needed.

24.2 External links

http://developer.android.com/reference/android/widget/ListView.html

Hack 25 *Creating fast adapters with a ViewHolder*
Android v1.6+

If you've already been programming in Android, you've probably used the Adapter class. But for those of you who haven't used the Adapter, it's described in the Android documentation (see section 25.2) as follows:

An `Adapter` object acts as a bridge between an `AdapterView` and the underlying data for that view. The `Adapter` provides access to the data items. The `Adapter` is also responsible for making a `View` for each item in the data set.

In this hack, I'll provide a short introduction on how the `Adapter` works so you can learn how to construct one quickly, making your application as responsive as possible.

The `AdapterView` is the abstract class for views that use an `Adapter` to fill themselves. A common subclass is the `ListView`. Both classes work together in a simple way. When the `AdapterView` is shown, it calls the `Adapter`'s `getView()` method to create and add the views as children. The `Adapter` will take care of creating the views in its `getView()` method. As you can imagine, instead of returning new views per row, Android offers a way to recycle them. Let's first look at how this works and then how to take advantage of the recycling.

In figure 25.1, we see a recycling example in action. In A we see the list loaded for the first time. In B the user scrolls down and the view for Item 1 disappears—instead of freeing the memory, it's sent to the recycler. When the `AdapterView` asks the `Adapter` for the next view, the `getView()` method is called and we get a recycled view in the `convertView` parameter. This way if Item 5's view is the same as Item 1's view, we can change the text and return it. The populated row will end in the empty space in C.

To explain this in a few words, when `getView()` is called, if `convertView` isn't null, then we use `convertView` instead of creating a new view. We need to fetch each widget's reference using `convertView.findViewById()` and populate it with the information from the model corresponding to the position.

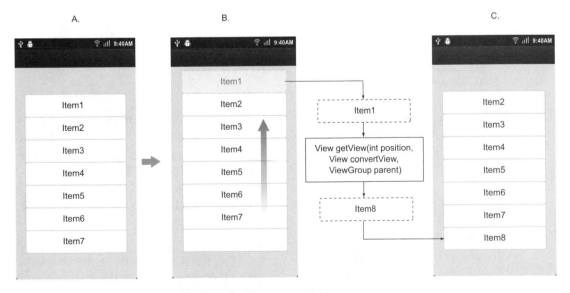

Figure 25.1   Views being recycled by the `Adapter`

Although this will work, we can tweak it further. To do so, we'll use the `ViewHolder` pattern. The `ViewHolder` is a static class where we can save the row's widgets to avoid the `findViewById()` calls every time `getView()` is called.

Let's see an example of how it's used. In the example, we'll create an `Adapter` that inflates a view that has an `ImageView` and two `TextViews`. The code follows:

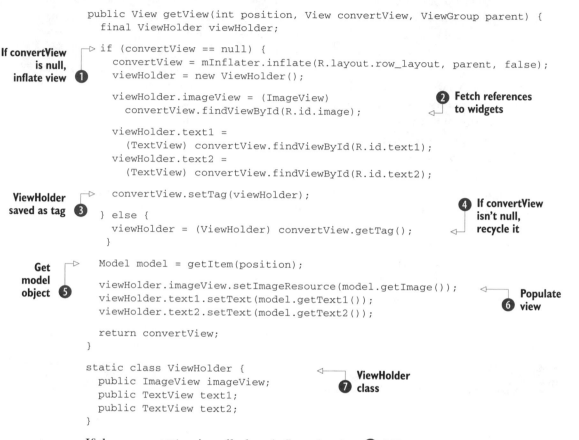

```
public View getView(int position, View convertView, ViewGroup parent) {
    final ViewHolder viewHolder;

    if (convertView == null) {
        convertView = mInflater.inflate(R.layout.row_layout, parent, false);
        viewHolder = new ViewHolder();

        viewHolder.imageView = (ImageView)
          convertView.findViewById(R.id.image);

        viewHolder.text1 =
          (TextView) convertView.findViewById(R.id.text1);
        viewHolder.text2 =
          (TextView) convertView.findViewById(R.id.text2);

        convertView.setTag(viewHolder);
    } else {
        viewHolder = (ViewHolder) convertView.getTag();
    }

    Model model = getItem(position);

    viewHolder.imageView.setImageResource(model.getImage());
    viewHolder.text1.setText(model.getText1());
    viewHolder.text2.setText(model.getText2());

    return convertView;
}

static class ViewHolder {
    public ImageView imageView;
    public TextView text1;
    public TextView text2;
}
```

If convertView is null, inflate view ❶

❷ Fetch references to widgets

ViewHolder saved as tag ❸

❹ If convertView isn't null, recycle it

Get model object ❺

❻ Populate view

❼ ViewHolder class

If the `convertView` is null, then inflate the view ❶. When we create the view, we need to fetch the references to the widgets and save them inside the `ViewHolder` ❷. The `ViewHolder` gets saved as a tag ❸. If the `convertView` isn't null, that means we can recycle it. We can get the `ViewHolder` from the `convertView`'s tag ❹. Then we get the model object, depending on the position ❺, and populate the view with information from the model ❻. The `ViewHolder` class contains all of the widgets as public fields ❼.

25.1 *The bottom line*

Almost every Android application uses some sort of list or gallery to present data. Because these kinds of widgets are subclasses of `AdapterView`, understanding how `AdapterView` works and how it interacts with an adapter is critical to making your application faster. The `ViewHolder` hack is an excellent way to achieve speed within lists.

25.2 External links

http://developer.android.com/reference/android/widget/Adapter.html
http://developer.android.com/training/improving-layouts/smooth-scrolling.html

Hack 26 *Adding section headers to a ListView*
Android v1.6+
Contributed by Chris King

Imagine that you want to create a vacation-planning application that allows users to browse a list of popular destinations organized by country. To present a long list of data, you'll want to include section information to help orient people within the list. For example, contacts applications will often group users by the first letter of their last name, and scheduling applications will group appointments by dates. You can accomplish this with a design similar to that used in the iPhone contacts screen, where a section header scrolls with the list, with the current section's header always visible at the top of the screen. In figure 26.1, the highlighted letters are the section headers, and the lists below them contain the countries whose name begins with those letters. What you see in the figure is difficult to create in Android because `ListView` doesn't have a concept of a section or a section header, only of items within the list.

Android developers often try to solve this problem by creating two types of list items: a regular item for data, and a separate item for section headers. We can do this by overriding the `getViewTypeCount()` method to return 2, and modifying our `getView()` method to create and return the appropriate type of item. In practice, however, this will lead to messy code. If our underlying list of data contains 20 items, our adapter will need to contain anywhere from 21 to 40 items, depending on how many sections it contains. This can lead to complicated code: the List-View might want to show the 15th visible item, which might be the 9th item in the underlying list.

A much simpler approach is to embed the section header within the list item, and then make it visible or invisible as needed. This greatly simplifies the logic for building the list and looking up items when

Figure 26.1 A sectioned list of country names

the user makes a selection. We can create a special `TextView` that overlaps the top of the list, and update it when the list scrolls a new section into view.

26.1 *Creating list layouts*

To create an experience like that shown in the previous figure, start by writing the following XML for the section header *R*, the third header shown in the previous image. We'll create this in a separate layout file so we can reuse it for headers that scroll with the list and the stationary header at the top:

```
<?xml version="1.0" encoding="utf-8"?>
<TextView xmlns:android="http://schemas.android.com/apk/res/android"
    android:id="@+id/header"
    style="@android:style/TextAppearance.Small"
    android:layout_width="fill_parent"
    android:layout_height="wrap_content"
    android:background="#0000ff" />
```

❶ Custom background color

The text has a custom background color ❶ to distinguish it from regular text in the list. Now, write the following XML for the screen, including the stationary section header:

```
<?xml version="1.0" encoding="utf-8"?>
<FrameLayout xmlns:android="http://schemas.android.com/apk/res/android"
    android:layout_width="fill_parent"
    android:layout_height="fill_parent">

    <ListView
        android:id="@android:id/list"
        android:layout_width="fill_parent"
        android:layout_height="fill_parent"/>

    <include layout="@layout/header"/>
</FrameLayout>
```

❶ Uses standard Android list ID

The list ❶ uses the standard Android list ID so we can use it in our subclass of `List-Activity`. Include the header in this frame, so it will overlap the list and show the current section.

The last XML to create is the list item, which follows, and includes both the data field and the section header:

```
<?xml version="1.0" encoding="utf-8"?>
<LinearLayout xmlns:android="http://schemas.android.com/apk/res/android"
    android:orientation="vertical"
    android:layout_width="fill_parent"
    android:layout_height="wrap_content">

    <include layout="@layout/header"/>

    <TextView
        android:id="@+id/label"
        style="@android:style/TextAppearance.Large"
        android:layout_width="fill_parent"
        android:layout_height="wrap_content"/>
</LinearLayout>
```

❶ Visible sections headers

❷ Shows data for the slot

Our section header ❶ will be visible for items that start a new section, and are hidden otherwise. The label ❷ will always show the data for this slot. The relationships between item, header, and label are shown in figure 26.2.

Figure 26.2   List items with label and optional header

26.2   *Providing visible section headers*

Next, create an `Adapter` subclass that will configure the list items. Unlike other approaches to creating a sectioned list, only `getView()` needs to be overridden; we don't need to return multiple types of views or convert between positions in the visible list and positions in the underlying data list:

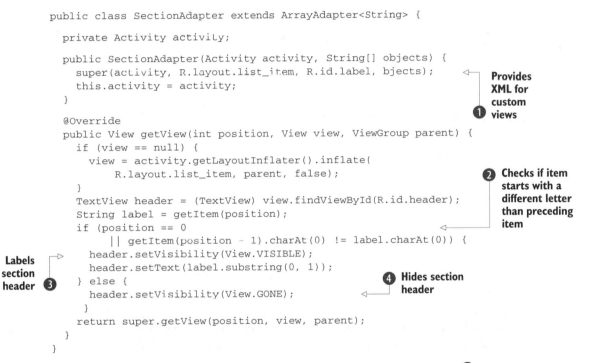

```
public class SectionAdapter extends ArrayAdapter<String> {

  private Activity activity;

  public SectionAdapter(Activity activity, String[] objects) {
    super(activity, R.layout.list_item, R.id.label, bjects);      ◁── Provides
    this.activity = activity;                                          XML for
  }                                                                    custom
                                                                     ❶ views
  @Override
  public View getView(int position, View view, ViewGroup parent) {
    if (view == null) {
      view = activity.getLayoutInflater().inflate(
          R.layout.list_item, parent, false);                     ❷ Checks if item
    }                                                                starts with a
    TextView header = (TextView) view.findViewById(R.id.header);     different letter
    String label = getItem(position);                                than preceding
    if (position == 0                                                 item
        || getItem(position - 1).charAt(0) != label.charAt(0)) {  ◁──┘
      header.setVisibility(View.VISIBLE);
      header.setText(label.substring(0, 1));
    } else {                                                      ❹ Hides section
      header.setVisibility(View.GONE);                         ◁──┘  header
    }
    return super.getView(position, view, parent);
  }
}
```

Labels section header ❸

The `ArrayAdapter` parent class can do most of the work if we provide ❶ the XML for its custom views. After creating a list item, check to see whether it starts with a different letter than the preceding item ❷. If it does, then it's the first item in this section, and so we label the section header and make it visible ❸. Otherwise, we hide it ❹.

Now that the section headers within the list are properly set, write a helper method that will configure the floating section header at the top of the screen:

```
private TextView topHeader;          ◁──❶ Accesses section header

...

private void setTopHeader(int pos) {
  final String text = Countries.COUNTRIES[pos].substring(0, 1);
```

```
   topHeader.setText(text);          ←── ❷ Updates text
 }
```

The instance variable ❶ lets us access the section header at the top of the screen. When we initially create or scroll the list, we'll call this helper method, which finds the appropriate letter to use for this section and updates the text ❷.

26.3 Wrapping up

Finally, bring it all together in the Activity's onCreate() method. Configure the list and attach a new listener that updates the header when the list scrolls:

```
private int topVisiblePosition;
...
public void onCreate(Bundle savedInstanceState) {
  super.onCreate(savedInstanceState);
  setContentView(R.layout.list);                           ❶ Attaches a
  topHeader = (TextView) findViewById(R.id.top);      ←──┘    scroll listener
  setListAdapter(new SectionAdapter(this, Countries.COUNTRIES));
  getListView().setOnScrollListener(new AbsListView.OnScrollListener() {
    @Override
    public void onScrollStateChanged(AbsListView view,
      int scrollState) {
      // Empty.
    }
    @Override
    public void onScroll(AbsListView view, int firstVisibleItem,
        int visibleItemCount, int totalItemCount) {
      if (firstVisibleItem != topVisiblePosition) {
        topVisiblePosition = firstVisibleItem;               ❷ Invokes the
        setTopHeader(firstVisibleItem);                   ←──┘   helper method
      }
    }                              ❸ Initializes first
  });                                  header to the
  setTopHeader(0);               ←──┘  first item
}
```

After configuring the UI ❶, attach a scroll listener. When users scroll the list, check to see whether they've changed position, and if so, invoke the helper method ❷ to update the floating header. Make sure to initialize the header to the first item ❸ when the list first appears.

26.4 The bottom line

Even though ListView doesn't automatically support section headers, you can easily add them by embedding the headers within your list items and making them visible or hidden as appropriate. Although this hack's example applies to an alphabetized list, the same approach can work for any type of sectioned grouping you'd like to create.

26.5 External links

http://developer.android.com/reference/android/widget/ListView.html
http://developer.android.com/reference/android/widget/BaseAdapter.html

Hack 27 *Communicating with an Adapter using an Activity and a delegate*
Android v1.6+

A lot of Android widgets use an `Adapter` to populate themselves. Every Android widget that uses an undefined list of views will have an `Adapter` to fetch them. This means that after you learn how to use one, you'll be able to operate a wide range of widgets easily. One benefit of this approach is that you can place all of the code related to the visual logic inside the `Adapter`. Why is this important? Because you can apply the concept of separation of concerns (SoC). Imagine that you need to show a list of telephone numbers with two different clickable widgets inside each row—the first one to remove the telephone number from the list, and the second one to make the call. Where would you place all of those click handlers?

In this hack, we'll look at how to solve this problem using the Delegation pattern. This pattern will help us to move all of the business logic away from the `Adapter` and place it inside the `Activity`. We'll create a simple application that adds numbers to a list and each row will have a Remove button to remove the phone number.

The idea is simple: we'll add the Remove button click handler in the `Adapter`, but instead of removing the object there, we'll call an `Activity`'s method through the delegate interface. The first thing we'll create is the `Adapter`'s code:

```
public class NumbersAdapter extends ArrayAdapter<Integer> {

  public static interface NumbersAdapterDelegate {         Defines
    void removeItem(Integer value);                         delegate
  }                                                       ① interface

  private LayoutInflater mInflator;
  private NumbersAdapterDelegate mDelegate;

  public NumbersAdapter(Context context, List<Integer> objects) {
    super(context, 0, objects);
    mInflator = LayoutInflater.from(context);
  }

  @Override
  public View getView(int position, View cv, ViewGroup parent) {

    if ( null == cv ) {
      cv = mInflator.inflate(R.layout.number_row, parent, false);
    }

    final Integer value = getItem(position);
    TextView tv = (TextView) cv.findViewById(R.id.numbers_row_text);
    tv.setText(value.toString());

    View button = cv.findViewById(R.id.numbers_row_button);
    button.setOnClickListener(new OnClickListener() {

      @Override
      public void onClick(View v) {
```

```
            if ( null != mDelegate ) {
                mDelegate.removeItem(value);
            }
        }
    });

    return cv;
}

public void setDelegate(NumbersAdapterDelegate delegate) {
    mDelegate = delegate;
}

}
```

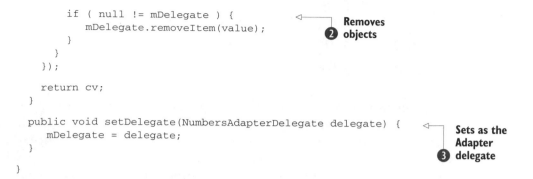

We define the delegate interface ❶ that will be used to handle removing the object ❷. The `Activity` will need a way to set itself as the `Adapter` delegate, and for that we have a setter ❸.

Now that we have the `Adapter` in place, let's take a look at the `Activity` code:

```
public class MainActivity extends Activity implements
    NumbersAdapterDelegate {

    private ListView mListView;
    private ArrayList<Integer> mNumbers;
    private NumbersAdapter mAdapter;

    @Override
    public void onCreate(Bundle savedInstanceState) {
        super.onCreate(savedInstanceState);
        setContentView(R.layout.main);

        mListView = (ListView) findViewById(R.id.main_listview);
        mNumbers = new ArrayList<Integer>();
        mAdapter = new NumbersAdapter(this, mNumbers);
        mListView.setAdapter(mAdapter);
    }

    @Override
    protected void onResume() {
        super.onResume();
        mAdapter.setDelegate(this);
    }

    @Override
    protected void onPause() {
        super.onPause();
        mAdapter.setDelegate(null);
    }

    @Override
    public void removeItem(Integer value) {
        mNumbers.remove(value);
        mAdapter.notifyDataSetChanged();
    }
}
```

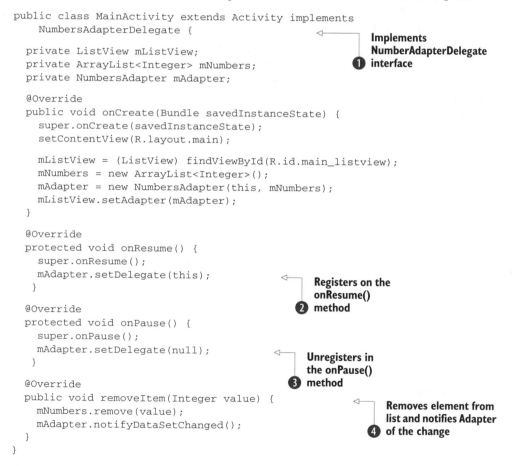

As you can see, the `Activity` implements the `NumbersAdapterDelegate` interface ❶. Instead of setting the `Activity` as the `Adapter`'s delegate inside the `onCreate()`

method, we register it in the onResume() method ❷ and unregister it in the
onPause() method ❸. We do this to be sure that the Activity is used as delegate
when it's shown in the screen. You can look at the delegate method ❹, which removes
the element from the list and notifies the Adapter of the change.

27.1 The bottom line

The Delegation pattern is used a lot in iOS development. For instance, when you create an HTTP request, you can set a delegate to determine what to do when the request
is finished. While coding for an iPhone application, I noticed that using the delegate
organized my code.

This example is only the tip of the iceberg. The Delegation pattern can be used in
lots of places in Android development. For example, you can also use Delegation to
take actions depending on an HTTP request. Keep in mind that it exists and use it
when it makes sense.

27.2 External links

http://en.wikipedia.org/wiki/Separation_of_concerns
http://en.wikipedia.org/wiki/Delegation_pattern

Hack 28 *Taking advantage of ListView's header*
Android v1.6+

Sometimes as developers we need to achieve weird
layouts based on a designer's wireframes. Some
months ago, I was involved with a project where the
wireframes had an image gallery on top and a list of
items on the bottom. It sounds simple—I placed an
Android Gallery and a ListView below it—but when
the designer saw the application running he came to
me and said, "I'd like to be able to scroll down to the
point where the gallery disappears."

In this hack, I'll show how I created what the
designer wanted: a gallery of images and a list of numbers where you can scroll down until the gallery disappears. The finished application can be seen in
figure 28.1.

To do this kind of layout, you might be tempted to
place the Gallery and ListView inside a ScrollView,

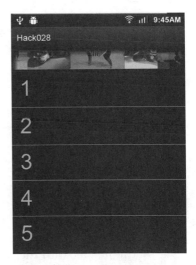

Figure 28.1 Demo application

but this wouldn't work because a ListView is already a ScrollView. You can try it out, but you'll run into issues because the ListView already handles scrolling.

Fortunately, the ListView provides methods to add custom headers and footers to it. Let's look at the following code to see how to use those methods to place the Gallery as a ListView's header:

```
public class MainActivity extends Activity {

  private static final String[] NUMBERS = {"1", "2", "3", "4",
    "5", "6", "7", "8"};
  private Gallery mGallery;
  private View mHeader;
  private ListView mListView;

  @Override
  public void onCreate(Bundle savedInstanceState) {
    super.onCreate(savedInstanceState);
    setContentView(R.layout.main);

    mListView = (ListView) findViewById(R.id.main_listview);      ❶ References
                                                                     the ListView

    LayoutInflater inflator = LayoutInflater.from(this);
    mHeader = inflator.inflate(R.layout.header, mListView, false);
    mGallery = (Gallery) mHeader.findViewById(R.id.gallery);
    mGallery.setAdapter(new ImageAdapter(this));

    ListView.LayoutParams params =
        new ListView.LayoutParams(ListView.LayoutParams.FILL_PARENT,
          ListView.LayoutParams.WRAP_CONTENT);
    mHeader.setLayoutParams(params);                          ❹ Adds the whole header
    mListView.addHeaderView(mHeader, null, false);              view to ListView

    ArrayAdapter<String> adapter =
        new ArrayAdapter<String>(this, R.layout.list_item, NUMBERS);
    mListView.setAdapter(adapter);

    mListView.setOnItemClickListener(                ❻ Adds an
      new OnItemClickListener() {                       onItemClick listener

        @Override
        public void onItemClick(AdapterView<?> parent, View view,
          int position, long id) {
          mGallery.setSelection(position-1);
        }
      });
  }
}
```

Creates different XML file that needs to be inflated ❷

Replaces original LayoutParams from header ❸

Sets the adapter to ListView ❺

The code provides a reference to the ListView ❶. This ListView will take the whole screen. For the header, we created a different XML file that needs to get inflated ❷. You can see that we make a second call to findViewById() inside the header view because we created a LinearLayout with the Gallery inside. It's not needed, but we might add something else in the future. We replace the original LayoutParams from the header with the ListView version ❸ and then add the whole header view to the ListView ❹. After setting the header, we set the adapter to the ListView ❺ and, finally, we add an `onItemClick` listener ❻ that will take care of scrolling the images inside the gallery every time we hover over a number.

28.1 The bottom line

Translating wireframes to real applications is hard—even more so when designers don't know about the platform limitations or its possibilities. The developer might end up hacking Android's code to make it as similar as possible. My best advice for this kind of situation is to try to get a good understanding of the framework and take it to the limit.

28.2 External links

http://developer.android.com/reference/android/widget/ListView.html

http://groups.google.com/group/android-beginners/browse_thread/thread/
   2d1a4b8063b2d8f7

Hack 29 Handling orientation changes inside a ViewPager
Android v1.6+

With the release of Compatibility Package revision 3, the `ViewPager` class was made available. If you've never used the `ViewPager` class, you should know it's an implementation of a horizontal view swiper. What's possible with the `ViewPager` class? You can create any kind of application that requires paginated views. The best part is that it works like an `AdapterView`, meaning that you use it as you'd use a `ListView`—simple.

Imagine you want to create a magazine-like application. Although the `ViewPager` class is an excellent ally to help you achieve this, it's hard to handle different orientation changes depending on the page. In this hack I'll show you how to use the `View-Pager` class and configure everything to make it work correctly.

For this hack, we'll create a color viewer application. We'll be able to swipe through colors and every page where (`index % 2`) `== 0` will have a landscape version available. To create this we'll need the following:

- An `Activity` that will hold the `ViewPager` and control the orientation changes
- A `ColorFragment` class that will show a color and some text in the middle of the screen
- A `ColorAdapter` class that will be in charge of creating the fragments and telling the `Activity` which fragment will be able to change the orientation configuration
- A `ViewPager` that will use the `ColorAdapter` to display our fragments

Let's look at the `Activity` code to see how to do this:

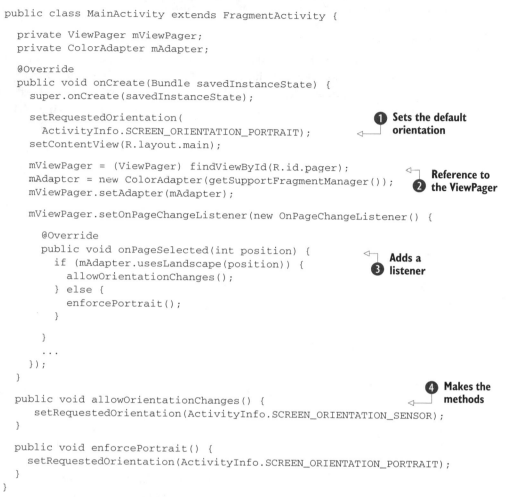

```java
public class MainActivity extends FragmentActivity {

  private ViewPager mViewPager;
  private ColorAdapter mAdapter;

  @Override
  public void onCreate(Bundle savedInstanceState) {
    super.onCreate(savedInstanceState);

    setRequestedOrientation(                              ❶ Sets the default
      ActivityInfo.SCREEN_ORIENTATION_PORTRAIT);            orientation
    setContentView(R.layout.main);

    mViewPager = (ViewPager) findViewById(R.id.pager);
    mAdapter = new ColorAdapter(getSupportFragmentManager());   ❷ Reference to
    mViewPager.setAdapter(mAdapter);                              the ViewPager

    mViewPager.setOnPageChangeListener(new OnPageChangeListener() {

      @Override
      public void onPageSelected(int position) {
        if (mAdapter.usesLandscape(position)) {          ❸ Adds a
          allowOrientationChanges();                        listener
        } else {
          enforcePortrait();
        }
      }
      ...
    });
  }
                                                         ❹ Makes the
  public void allowOrientationChanges() {                   methods
    setRequestedOrientation(ActivityInfo.SCREEN_ORIENTATION_SENSOR);
  }

  public void enforcePortrait() {
    setRequestedOrientation(ActivityInfo.SCREEN_ORIENTATION_PORTRAIT);
  }
}
```

The first thing to do is set the default orientation to portrait ❶. This means that if the view doesn't specify whether it allows orientation changes, it'll stay portrait. The code provides a reference to the `ViewPager` ❷, and we'll set the `ColorAdapter` to it. Add a listener ❸ when the page is changed, and inside it ask the `Adapter` whether to allow orientation changes. Finally, make the methods ❹ that take care of enabling or disabling the orientation changes using the `setRequestedOrientation()` method that comes from the `Activity`.

29.1   *The bottom line*

The `ViewPager` class brought a standardized implementation of a horizontal view swiper to Android, and the best thing is that it's backward compatible to API level 4, which is Android 1.6. If you've never used it, try it out; it's a nice tool to have.

On the other hand, in this hack you saw how to limit orientation changes in your views. Remember that it's always better to support both orientations for every view. Your users will appreciate it if you allow them to position the device in different ways when using your application.

29.2   *External links*

http://android-developers.blogspot.com/2011/08/horizontal-view-swiping-with-view-pager.html

http://developer.android.com/sdk/compatibility-library.html

Hack 30   *ListView's choiceMode*
Android v1.6+

Android's `ListView` is one of the most important classes in the SDK. Apart from showing items in a scrollable list, it can also be used to pick stuff from that list. Imagine you need to create an `Activity` to let your user pick a country from a list. How would you do it? Would you handle the selection yourself? You could create a `ListView` and handle the selection yourself using click handlers, but in this hack I'll provide a better way to do it.

In this hack, you'll learn how to use a `ListView` to create a country picker. An example of this picker is shown in figure 30.1. When a country row is selected and you click on the Pick Country button, a `Toast` will be shown with the country name.

The `ListView` has something called `choiceMode`. In the documentation (see section 30.2), you'll see the following explanation:

> Defines the choice behavior for the view. By default, lists do not have any choice behavior. By setting the `choiceMode` to `singleChoice`, the list allows up to one item to be in a chosen state. By setting the `choiceMode` to `multipleChoice`, the list allows any number of items to be chosen.

In this case, we'll use `singleChoice` as the `choiceMode`, but if we wanted to pick several items from the list we'd use `multipleChoice`.

Figure 30.1   Country picker

Another interesting feature of the ListView widget is that whether we use single-Choice or multipleChoice, they automatically save the selected position(s). You already know that the ListView will help us create the picker by setting the choice-Mode to singleChoice. Let's create the Activity's layout:

```
<LinearLayout xmlns:android="http://schemas.android.com/apk/res/android"
    xmlns:tools="http://schemas.android.com/tools"
    android:layout_width="fill_parent"
    android:layout_height="fill_parent"
    android:orientation="vertical" >

    <Button
        android:layout_width="fill_parent"
        android:layout_height="wrap_content"
        android:onClick="onPickCountryClick"
        android:text="@string/activity_main_add_selection" />

    <ListView
        android:id="@+id/activity_main_list"
        android:layout_width="fill_parent"
        android:layout_height="fill_parent"
        android:choiceMode="singleChoice" />

</LinearLayout>
```

❶ Uses a Button to execute the method

❷ Shows the country list

The layout is simple. We'll use a Button ❶ to execute the method that handles the logic of retrieving the selected country, and a ListView with singleChoice ❷ to show the country list.

Now let's create the custom row layout and the Activity source code. The row layout will use the following code:

```
<LinearLayout xmlns:android="http://schemas.android.com/apk/res/android"
    xmlns:tools="http://schemas.android.com/tools"
    android:layout_width="fill_parent"
    android:layout_height="wrap_content"
    android:orientation="horizontal" >

    <TextView
        android:id="@+id/country_view_title"
        android:layout_width="0dp"
        android:layout_height="wrap_content"
        android:layout_weight="0.9"
        android:padding="10dp" />

    <CheckBox
        android:id="@+id/country_view_checkbox"
        android:layout_width="0dp"
        android:layout_height="wrap_content"
        android:layout_weight="0.1"
        android:gravity="center_vertical"
        android:padding="10dp" />

</LinearLayout>
```

The Activity will have the following code:

```
public class MainActivity extends Activity {
  private ListView mListView;
  private CountryAdapter mAdapter;
  private ListCountry mCountries;
  private String mToastFmt;

  @Override
  public void onCreate(Bundle savedInstanceState) {
    super.onCreate(savedInstanceState);
    setContentView(R.layout.activity_main);

    createCountriesList();

    mToastFmt = getString(R.string.activity_main_toast_fmt);
    mAdapter = new CountryAdapter(this, -1, mCountries);
    mListView = (ListView)
      findViewById(R.id.activity_main_list);
    mListView.setAdapter(mAdapter);
  }

  public void onPickCountryClick(View v) {
    int pos = mListView.getCheckedItemPosition();

    if (ListView.INVALID_POSITION != pos) {
      String msg = String.format(mToastFmt, mCountries.get(pos)
        .getName());
      Toast.makeText(this, msg, Toast.LENGTH_SHORT).show();
    }
  }
}
```

Helper method to populate list of countries ← (annotation pointing to `createCountriesList();`)

Create an Adapter and set it to ListView ← (annotation pointing to `mListView.setAdapter(mAdapter);`)

If something is selected, show a Toast with country name ← (annotation pointing to the `if` block)

Sounds simple so far, right? It is, but there's a trick to using it. We need to understand how the ListView sets a position to be checked or not to use it correctly.

If you stop reading this and search the web looking for code samples about the ListView's choiceMode, you'll notice that most of the results use a class called CheckedTextView for the row view, instead of a custom view as we did. If you look for the source code of that class, you'll notice that it's an extension of the TextView class, which implements the Checkable interface.

So the ListView is somehow using the Checkable interface to handle the view state. If you browse the ListView source code, you'll find the following:

```
if (mChoiceMode != CHOICE_MODE_NONE && mCheckStates != null) {
  if (child instanceof Checkable) {
    ((Checkable) child).setChecked(mCheckStates.get(position));
  }
}
```

We need to make our custom row implement the Checkable interface if we want the ListView to handle the selection. Unfortunately, this is only possible when creating a custom view. Let's create a class called CountryView. The code is the following:

```
public class CountryView extends LinearLayout
  implements Checkable {

  private TextView mTitle;
```

```
          private CheckBox mCheckBox;

          public CountryView(Context context, AttributeSet attrs) {
            super(context, attrs);
            LayoutInflater inflater = LayoutInflater.from(context);
            View v = inflater.inflate(R.layout.country_view, this, true);
            mTitle = (TextView) v.findViewById(R.id.country_view_title);
            mCheckBox = (CheckBox) v.findViewById(R.id.country_view_checkbox);
          }

          public void setTitle(String title) {
            mTitle.setText(title);
          }

          @Override
          public boolean isChecked() {
            return mCheckBox.isChecked();
          }

          @Override
          public void setChecked(boolean checked) {
            mCheckBox.setChecked(checked);
          }

          @Override
          public void toggle() {
            mCheckBox.toggle();
          }
        }
```

Inflate the layout (annotation pointing to the `LayoutInflater`/`View v = inflater.inflate` lines)

Override all the Checkable methods (annotation pointing to the `isChecked()` method)

Notice how the Checkable interface methods are implemented. Every method calls the mCheckBox implementation. This means that when the ListView wants to select a row it will call the CountryView's setChecked() method.

Everything is set. We can now run the application. You'll notice that when you click on a row, the CheckBox won't be ticked, but if you click over the CheckBox it is. You might also be able to check a row and when you scroll, you might see rows getting selected. What's wrong?

The issue is that we're adding a focusable widget, the CheckBox. The best way to solve this is to disallow the CheckBox to gain focus. And, because the ListView is the one that decides what should and shouldn't be checked, we'll also remove the CheckBox possibility of getting clicks. We do this by adding the following attributes to the XML:

```
android:clickable="false"
android:focusable="false"
android:focusableInTouchMode="false"
```

If we run the application now with this modification, everything will work as we'd expect.

30.1   *The bottom line*

This hack solves another issue brought on by the lack of Android documentation. Using the ListView's choiceMode correctly requires reading the SDK source code, but when you understand how it works, it's a great feature to use when you need to pick one or several items from a list.

30.2 External links

http://developer.android.com/reference/android/widget/
    AbsListView.html#attr_android:choiceMode

http://stackoverflow.com/questions/5612600/
    listview-with-choice-mode-multiple-using-checkedtext-in-a-custom-view

Useful libraries

In this chapter, we'll cover two third-party libraries. The first one lets you use aspect-oriented programming inside an Android application. The second is a game framework. We'll walk through what's possible when you add them to your application.

Hack 31 *Aspect-oriented programming in Android*
Android v1.6+

Have you ever tried to add analytics, ads, and logs to an Android `Activity`? If you have, you know that your class can get polluted with a lot of code that has nothing to do with your `Activity`'s logic. In this hack, you'll see how to solve this issue using aspect-oriented programming (AOP). As an example, we'll add a log statement to the `Activity`'s `onCreate()` method using AOP to make sure that the `Activity` doesn't get polluted.

Aspect-oriented programming is a programming paradigm that aims to increase modularity by allowing the separation of cross-cutting concerns. Here's a basic idea of how all of this works: we specify our cross-cutting concerns in a separated module (aspect), and we place the code that we want to be executed (either before or after our cross-cutting concern) in the separate module or modules. Figure 31.1 illustrates this concept.

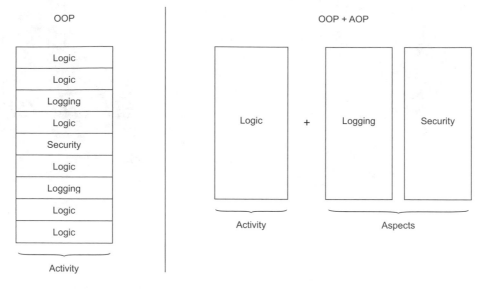

Figure 31.1 AOP modularity

Inside Android, AOP can be implemented using a library called AspectJ. Since Android doesn't support bytecode generation, we can't use all the AspectJ features. One AspectJ feature that works in Android is called *compile-time weaving*. To understand how this works, you first need to understand when it happens. AspectJ will modify our code after it's compiled to bytecode and before it's converted to dex. There it'll take care of adding the additional code to our cross-cutting concerns. See figure 31.2.

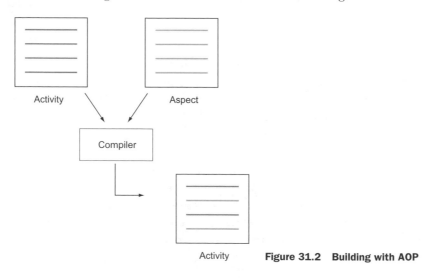

Figure 31.2 Building with AOP

To make AOP work, we'll need to modify the build procedure. In this case, we'll use Apache Maven because then we only need to add some dependencies to a pom.xml, and a build plugin makes everything extremely simple.

The Apache Maven plugin we'll use is called `aspectj-maven plugin`

Let's take a look at the `aspectj-maven-plugin` configuration inside the pom.xml build section:

```
<plugin>
    <groupId>org.codehaus.mojo</groupId>
    <artifactId>aspectj-maven-plugin</artifactId>
    <version>1.4</version>
    <configuration>
        <source>1.5</source>
        <complianceLevel>1.5</complianceLevel>
        <showWeaveInfo>true</showWeaveInfo>          ◁──❶ showWeaveInfo on
        <verbose>true</verbose>              ◁──❷ verbose on
    </configuration>
    <executions>
        <execution>
        <goals>
            <goal>compile</goal>             ◁──❸ goal is set to compile
        </goals>
        </execution>
    </executions>
</plugin>
```

While developing aspects, turn the `showWeaveInfo` ❶ and `verbose` ❷ flags on. This will log information about the weaving process, helping us understand how everything gets applied. Using `compile` ❸ as `goal` tells the plugin to weave all the main classes. If we need to weave our test classes as well, we'll need to add `<goal>test-compile</goal>`.

Because we didn't specify a path for the code, the AspectJ plugin will look for files inside the src/main/ directory. There we'll create a java directory for the Java source code and an aspect folder for the aspects.

We've configured everything to start using AspectJ in our project. Because we want to clean our `Activity` from logs, we'll now create a log aspect. We have two possibilities for creating an aspect: the AspectJ language syntax and the @AspectJ annotation style. The big difference is that the language syntax should be easier to write aspects in, since it was purposefully designed for that, whereas the annotation style follows regular Java compilation. Because we're not doing something huge and our aspect is simple, we'll use the annotation style.

Inside the aspect folder is a file, LogAspect.java, that describes the aspect:

```
@Aspect                      ◁──❶ AspectJ annotation
public class LogAspect {

    @Pointcut("within(com.manning.androidhacks.hack031.MainActivity)")
    private void mainActivity() {       ◁─┐
    }                                      ❷ Pointcut for our Activity

    @Pointcut("execution(* onCreate(..))")   ◁─┐ Pointcut for the
                                               ❸ onCreate() method
```

```
         private void onCreate() {
         }
```

Pointcuts get mixed ④

```
         @AfterReturning(pointcut = "mainActivity() && onCreate()")
         public void logAfterOnCreateOnMainActivity() {
             Log.d("TAG", "OnCreate() has been called!");          ◁─── ⑤ Advice to run
         }
     }
```

If you haven't used AspectJ, here's a small reference for understanding the code:

- A *join point* is a well-defined point in the program flow.
- A *pointcut* picks out certain join points and values at those points.
- A piece of *advice* is code that's executed when a join point is reached.

Because we chose to use the annotation style, we'll need to annotate the class with @Aspect ❶. The first two methods from the class are annotated with @Pointcut. In this example, the first one creates a pointcut for our MainActivity ❷ class and the second one for any method that is called onCreate() ❸. The third method is an advice. Because we've annotated it with @AfterReturning, the advice runs when the matched method execution returns normally. Note how the mainActivity() and onCreate pointcuts are mixed with an && ❹. When you reach that join point, the advice code will get executed ❺.

There's more than one way to describe a join point. In the example, we mix two pointcuts, but you can easily find other ways of doing the same thing. Depending on what you want to achieve, you'll need to start playing with pointcuts and advices.

31.1 *The bottom line*

In this example, you saw how to use AspectJ's compile-time weaving to add logs to a method call inside an Activity, but imagine what's possible. Don't limit yourself to thinking that AOP is a way of moving lines of code to a different class. Go though your application design and analyze how this approach could improve your code modularity.

31.2 *External links*

http://en.wikipedia.org/wiki/Aspect-oriented_programming

http://eclipse.org/aspectj/doc/released/faq.php

http://mojo.codehaus.org/aspectj-maven-plugin/

http://williamd1618.blogspot.com/2011/04/
    android-and-aspect-oriented-programming.html

www.eclipse.org/aspectj/doc/next/progguide/starting-aspectj.html

Hack 32 *Empowering your application using Cocos2d-x*
Android V2.2+

Android provides different ways to present your application information to the user, but sometimes these might be insufficient. Imagine you want to add a graph view or a 3D animation to your application. How would you do that? Some developers might try using OpenGL for their views, but this means adding a layer of complexity, and not everyone knows how to code OpenGL.

In this hack, I'll show you to how use the game framework called Cocos2d-x to add an edge to your applications.

32.1 What is Cocos2d-x?

Cocos2d started as a Python game framework to be used in a competition called PyWeek. The name comes from a city in Córdoba, Argentina, called Los Cocos. Later on, Ricardo Quesada, one of the creators of Cocos2d, ported it to Objective-C and *Cocos2d for iPhone* was born. Cocos2d for iPhone is better known that the Python version and is used in a bunch of games in the Apple App Store. Did you ever play Zombie Smash! or Feed me Oil? These are examples of Cocos2d for iPhone games that reached number one in the top paid iPhone apps chart.

Cocos2d-x is a C++ port of the Cocos2d for iPhone game engine. It's a multiplatform, lightweight, developer-friendly, free, open source project and—guess what—it works in Android using the Android NDK.

32.2 Using Cocos2d-x

To show you what Cocos2d-x is capable of, we'll create a normal Android application and we'll make it snow. Using a particle system, we'll add a chilling visual effect to our view. The finished work can be seen in figure 32.1.

For starters, you should understand that Cocos2d-x uses OpenGL to draw everything. In Android, to draw OpenGL, the developer will need to use a Surface-View. Let's see how the SurfaceView works to understand how Cocos2d-x will get mixed into our application.

In the SurfaceView documentation (see section 32.4) we can read the following:

Figure 32.1 Application with a make-it-snow effect

The SurfaceView is a special subclass of View that offers a dedicated drawing surface within the View hierarchy. The aim is to offer this drawing surface to an application's secondary thread, so that the application isn't required to wait until the system's View hierarchy is ready to draw. Instead, a secondary thread that has reference to a SurfaceView can draw to its own Canvas at its own pace.

The last paragraph holds a lots of important information, so let me try to explain it in an easier way. Every time we add a widget or a custom view to our application, it gets added to the view hierarchy. Our complete tree of views (which forms our Activity) gets drawn in what's called the *UI thread*. On the other hand, the SurfaceView gets its own thread to draw and it won't use the UI thread. If the SurfaceView doesn't use the UI thread to draw itself, how docs Android deal with the mixture of the view hierarchy and surface views? To understand this, we must analyze the following paragraph (see section 32.4):

The surface is Z ordered so that it is behind the window holding its SurfaceView; the SurfaceView punches a hole in its window to allow its surface to be displayed. The view hierarchy will take care of correctly compositing with the Surface any siblings of the SurfaceView that would normally appear on top of it. This can be used to place overlays such as buttons on top of the Surface, though note however that it can have an impact on performance since a full alpha-blended composite will be performed each time the Surface changes.

The big conclusion we can get from this last paragraph is that we can mix both worlds but with certain restrictions. The SurfaceView will be placed in front of or in back of our view hierarchy. In our example, we'll have our view hierarchy in the back and will place the SurfaceView in front of it. So let's get started creating our view hierarchy first.

We'll first create the XML for our Activity. Here's the code:

```
<?xml version="1.0" encoding="utf-8"?>
<RelativeLayout
  xmlns:android="http://schemas.android.com/apk/res/android"
    android:layout_width="fill_parent"
    android:layout_height="fill_parent" >

    <TextView android:id="@+id/winter_text"
        android:layout_width="fill_parent"
        android:layout_height="wrap_content"
        android:layout_alignParentTop="true"
        android:layout_marginTop="5dp"
        android:gravity="center"
        android:text="Hello Winter!"
        android:textSize="30sp" />

    <View android:id="@+id/separator"
        android:layout_width="fill_parent"
        android:layout_height="5dp"
        android:layout_below="@id/winter_text"
```

```
        android:background="#FFFFFF" />

<TextView android:layout_width="fill_parent"
    android:layout_height="wrap_content"
    android:layout_centerInParent="true"
    android:layout_marginTop="5dp"
    android:gravity="center"
    android:text="It's snowing!"
    android:textSize="30sp" />

<FrameLayout android:layout_width="fill_parent"
        android:layout_height="fill_parent"
        android:layout_below="@id/separator">

    <org.cocos2dx.lib.Cocos2dxEditText
        android:id="@+id/game_edittext"
        android:layout_height="wrap_content"
        android:layout_width="fill_parent"
        android:background="@null"/>

    <org.cocos2dx.lib.Cocos2dxGLSurfaceView
        android:id="@+id/game_gl_surfaceview"
        android:layout_width="fill_parent"
        android:layout_height="fill_parent"/>
</FrameLayout>
</RelativeLayout>
```

- **❶ FrameLayout**
- **❷ Creates an org.coco2dx.lib .Cocos2dxEditText**
- **❸ Places SurfaceView inside the XML**

The layout has nothing special in it. I've organized the different views using a RelativeLayout. The interesting stuff is inside the FrameLayout ❶. We can first see how an org.cocos2dx.lib.Cocos2dxEditText is created ❷. The Cocos2dxEditText is needed by Cocos2d-x to show the keyboard when the game demands text input from the user. It's not something that we'll use, but it's required. The other important element is the SurfaceView ❸. Placing the SurfaceView inside the XML offers an unique way of positioning and providing a width and height to our Cocos2d-x's view. We could've used the whole screen, but I wanted to show you how we can use Android resources to place the SurfaceView on the screen without worrying about device sizes, pixel density, and so on.

Let's continue with the Activity's code. It's just copied and pasted from the Cocos2d-x Hello World sample application. Here's what it does:

```
public class MainActivity extends Cocos2dxActivity {
  private Cocos2dxGLSurfaceView mGLView;

  protected void onCreate(Bundle savedInstanceState) {
    super.onCreate(savedInstanceState);

    if (detectOpenGLES20()) {
      String packageName = getApplication().getPackageName();
      super.setPackageName(packageName);

      setContentView(R.layout.game_demo);
      mGLView = (Cocos2dxGLSurfaceView)
        findViewById(R.id.game_gl_surfaceview);
      Cocos2dxEditText edittext = (Cocos2dxEditText)
        findViewById(R.id.game_edittext);

      mGLView.setEGLContextClientVersion(2);
```

- **❶ Extends Cocos2dxActivity**
- **❷ Tells Cocos2d-x our application package**
- **❸ Informs Cocos2d-x where Cocos2dxEditText is**

```
        mGLView.setCocos2dxRenderer(new Cocos2dxRenderer());
        mGLView.setTextField(edittext);

    } else {
        Log.d("activity", "do not support gles2.0");
        finish();                                    ◁──────── ❶ Closes the app
    }
  }
}
```

To use Cocos2d-x features in our `Activity`, we need to extend `Cocos2dxActivity` ❶.
We tell Cocos2d-x our application package ❷. Cocos2d-x will use that package to read
assets from the Assets folder. We also inform Cocos2d-x where the `Cocos2dxEditText`
is ❸. If the device we're running doesn't support OpenGL 2.0, then we need to close
the app ❹.

    We'll also take the liberty of modifying Cocos2d-x's Java code to place the
`SurfaceView` on top of the view hierarchy and make its background translucent. To
do so, we add the following lines in the `initView()` method of the `Cocos2dxGL-
SurfaceView` class:

```
setEGLConfigChooser(8, 8, 8, 8, 16, 0);
getHolder().setFormat(PixelFormat.TRANSLUCENT);
setZOrderOnTop(true);
```

Also add the following line in the `onSurfaceCreated()` method of the
`Cocos2dxRenderer` class:

```
gl.glClearColor(0, 0, 0, 0);
```

We have all the Java code in place; we just need to write the C++ code to take care of
the snow. Since this is just an example of what's possible, I copied and pasted one of
Cocos2d-x's particle system tests that involves snow falling down. The code is all inside
the HelloWorldScene.cpp file that comes with the sample code for this book.

    If you've never used C++ in Android before, you should know that you need to use
the Android NDK.

32.3   *The bottom line*

Using Cocos2d-x is a great way to improve how your application looks and an excellent way to avoid dealing with OpenGL directly. Unfortunately you'll need to deal with
its limitations and its complexity. You'll need to write C++ code, deal with the NDK,
and set up your views to place a `SurfaceView` correctly, among other things. In the
end, it's totally worth the effort.

32.4 *External links*

http://developer.android.com/sdk/ndk/index.html

http://www.cocos2d-x.org/

http://developer.android.com/guide/topics/graphics/index.html#OnSurfaceView

http://www.cocos2d-iphone.org/archives/888

http://www.cocos2d-iphone.org/archives/1496

http://developer.android.com/guide/topics/graphics/2d-graphics.html

http://developer.android.com/reference/android/view/SurfaceView.html

Interacting with other languages

8

Android applications are coded mainly in Java. Officially, Android also supports C/C++ using the Android NDK (Native Development Kit). But is it possible to develop applications using other programming languages? In this chapter, we'll analyze the other possibilities.

Hack 33 Running Objective-C in Android
Android v1.6+

During the summer of 2011, my company released an iOS game called Shaman Doctor. The game was developed using cocos2d-iphone, an iOS library. The cocos2d-iphone library is coded in Objective-C, but there are a lot of forks that offer the same API in other programming languages. One of the most active forks is cocos2d-x. Instead of using Objective-C, cocos2d-x uses C++, and the most interesting thing about this project is that the API looks like Objective-C. To get an idea of what the Cocos2d-x team has created, take a look at the following code:

cocos2d-iphone version
```
[[SimpleAudioEngine sharedEngine] playEffect:@"sfx.file"];

SimpleAudioEngine::sharedEngine()->playEffect("sfx.file");
```
cocos2d-x version

As you might have noticed, the API is exactly the same, but to port a game from cocos2d-iphone to cocos2d-x you would need to port all your Objective-C code to C++, which is a boring task.

When I started looking for alternatives, I found a library called Itoa created by Dmitry Skiba. To understand what Itoa is capable of, let me quote its documentation (see section 33.5):

> [Itoa] is a cluster of open-source projects hosted on GitHub that implement compiler, build scripts and various libraries to allow building Android's apk from Objective-C source files.

Itoa's main purpose is more than just running Objective-C in Android; it's to magically convert an iOS application to an Android one. While its main feature is far from complete, the fact that it allows running Objective-C in Android is real.

What we'll do in this hack is port a simple Objective-C library called `Text-Formatter`. This means that we'll run the Objective-C code in Android without needing to modify it.

FOUNDATION: THE NDK AND OBJECTIVE-C   Itoa makes heavy use of the Android NDK. You'll need to understand how the NDK works to understand what comes next. If you have never used the Android NDK, you can read about it in *Android in Action, Third Edition* (W. Frank Ableson et al., Manning Publications, 2011). You'll also need to have a basic understanding of Objective-C.

33.1 *Downloading and compiling Itoa*

Compiling the Itoa library is quite easy. Just run the following from the command line:

```
wget https://github.com/downloads/DmitrySkiba/itoa/build-ndk.sh
chmod +X build-ndk.sh
./build-ndk.sh
```

This script will create a folder named itoa, fetch all subprojects, and build the NDK inside itoa/ndk. The resulting folder structure can be seen in figure 33.1. In other words, the script will first set up the tool chain and it'll use it to compile all the subprojects, leaving the .so files inside a folder at /itoa/ndk/itoa/platform/arch-arm/usr/lib.

33.2 *Creating the modules*

As in any ordinary NDK application, we'll separate the code in modules. We'll create a module called `text-`

Figure 33.1   Itoa folder structure

`formatter` containing the library we want to port, and a second one called `main`, which will be in charge of the communication between Java and the `TextFormatter` class.

33.2.1 *The ItoaApp.mk and the ItoaModule.mk files*

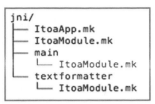

Figure 33.2   Jni folder structure

In a way similar to how the Android NDK uses the Application.mk and the Android.mk make files, Itoa has the ItoaApp.mk and the ItoaModule.mk files.

Inside our Android project directory, we'll create a folder called jni. This jni folder will contain two make files, ItoaApp.mk and ItoaModule.mk, and two folders to hold the modules—one folder for the textformatter module and a second one for the main module. Inside each module folder, we'll create an ItoaModule.mk file. The resulting directory structure can be seen in figure 33.2.

Let's take a look at what we'll place inside the ItoaApp.mk and ItoaModule.mk files. In the ItoaModule.mk make file, we'll point to the module's ItoaModule.mk files relative to the jni folder. The content is the following:

```
THIS_PATH := $(call my-dir)
include $(THIS_PATH)/main/ItoaModule.mk
include $(THIS_PATH)/TextFormatter/ItoaModule.mk
```

The ItoaApp.mk file contains more interesting information. The content is the following:

```
APP_IS_LIBRARY := true
 APP_LIBRARY_BIN_PATH = ../libs/$(TARGET_ABI)
```

1 Turn on library mode

2 Set path for .so files

The default settings for the ItoaApp.mk file are enough for what we want to create. Since we don't want to create an Android APK from the Objective-C code, we need to turn on the library mode **1**. The second setting is to set the path where the .so files will be saved **2**.

33.2.2 *The textformatter module*

The library to port is very simple. It only has a class method that returns an NSString *. The Objective-C code for this library is comprised of a .h file and a .m file. Here's the code:

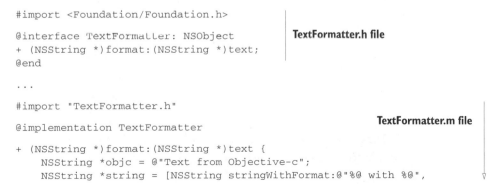

```
#import <Foundation/Foundation.h>

@interface TextFormatter: NSObject
+ (NSString *)format:(NSString *)text;
@end
```

TextFormatter.h file

```
...

#import "TextFormatter.h"

@implementation TextFormatter

+ (NSString *)format:(NSString *)text {
    NSString *objc = @"Text from Objective-c";
    NSString *string = [NSString stringWithFormat:@"%@ with %@",
```

TextFormatter.m file

```
        objc, text];

    return string;                          TextFormatter.m file
}

@end
```

As you can see, the library doesn't need any modification. It's just a .h and .m like you would use in an Objective-C application. Now let's see how to configure the ItoaModule.mk file to compile this. Itoa NDK build scripts were derived from Android NDK, but they were refactored. For example, the ItoaModule.mk file renames all the LOCAL_* variables to MODULE_*. The content of the make file is the following:

```
MODULE_PATH := $(call my-dir)
include $(CLEAR_VARS)

MODULE_NAME := textformatter               ◁──── Module name

MODULE_SRC_FILES := \
    TextFormatter.m                        ◁──── Source files to compile


MODULE_C_INCLUDES += \
    $(MODULE_PATH) \                       ◁──── Path to the include files


include $(BUILD_SHARED_LIBRARY)
```

Very similar to Android NDK make files, right?

33.2.3 *The main module*

The main module holds two source files:

- JNIOnLoad.cpp, where we'll use the JNI_OnLoad method
- main.mm, where we'll link JNI calls with the TextFormatter implementation

Let's create the JNIOnLoad.cpp file first:

```
#include <CoreFoundation/CFRuntime.h>
#include <jni.h>

extern "C"
{
jint JNI_OnLoad(JavaVM *vm, void *reserved) {

  _CFInitialize();                         ◁──── Initialize CoreFoundation

  extern void call_dyld_handlers();                ◁──── Load Objective-C classes
  call_dyld_handlers();

  return JNI_VERSION_1_6;
}
}
```

Because the virtual machine calls the JNI_OnLoad method when the native library is loaded, it's a great place to make the initialization needed by Itoa.

Now let's complete the main.mm implementation, which is the following:

```
#include <jni.h>
#import <Foundation/Foundation.h>
#import <objc/runtime.h>
#import <TextFormatter.h>

extern "C"
{
jstring
Java_com_manning_androidhacks_hack033_TextFormatter_formatString(
    JNIEnv* env, jobject thiz, jstring text)          ◁———  TextFormatter
 {                                                          ❶ JNI call
  jstring result = NULL;

  NSAutoreleasePool *pool = [NSAutoreleasePool new];
  const char *nativeText = env->GetStringUTFChars(text, 0);   ◁——  Convert
  NSString *objcText =                                              jstring to
    [NSString stringWithUTF8String:nativeText];                ❷ NSString *
  env->ReleaseStringUTFChars(text, nativeText);

  NSString *formattedText = [TextFormatter format: objcText];
  result =  env->NewStringUTF([formattedText UTF8String]);   ◁——  Return a
                                                                   jstring with
  [pool drain];                                              ❸ result

  return result;
 }
}
```

In the previous example, we have a mixture of C, C++, and Objective-C in the same file. From the method signature, we can learn that the `TextFormatter` Java native call will get a `String` as a parameter and will return a `String` ❶. Another interesting concept to learn here is that we can't send the `jstring` we get as a parameter to the `TextFormatter` implementation directly. We need to convert the `jstring` to a `char *` and then convert that `char *` to an `NSString *` ❷. After calling the `TextFormatter` implementation, we'll get an `NSString *` that will need to be converted to a `jstring`. This is done by converting it to `char *` first, and using the `env` to be able to return a `jstring` ❸.

The ItoaModule.mk file for main is the following:

```
MODULE_PATH := $(call my-dir)
include $(CLEAR_VARS)

MODULE_NAME := main                    ◁——— Module's name

MODULE_SRC_FILES := \
    JNIOnLoad.cpp \                    ◁——— Source files to compile
    main.mm \

MODULE_C_INCLUDES += \                         ◁——— Include TextFormatter.h path
        $(MODULE_PATH)/../textformatter \

MODULE_SHARED_LIBRARIES += textformatter      ◁——— textformatter dependency

include $(BUILD_SHARED_LIBRARY)
APP_SHARED_LIBRARIES += $(TARGET_ITOA_LIBRARIES)      ◁——❶ Add Itoa .so files
```

Let's talk about what the APP_SHARED_LIBRARIES is for ❶. For that variable, we used the macro $(TARGET_ITOA_LIBRARIES), which means that the .so files located at $ITOA_NDK/itoa/platform/arch-arm/usr/lib will be included in the libs directory. If you check what's inside that directory, you'll notice there are more .so files than we actually need. Before building it, you'll need to delete (or move) the following libraries from $ITOA_NDK/itoa/platform/arch-arm/usr/lib:

- libcg.so
- libcore.so
- libjnipp.so
- libuikit.so

33.2.4 *Compiling*

Now that we have all the native code in place, we need to compile all the .so files. Run this code

```
$ITOA_NDK/itoa-build
```

from the jni folder.

> **ITOA-BUILD -C** You can also use $ITOA_NDK/itoa-build -C /path/to/jni to avoid having to move to the jni folder.

After the compilation procedure finishes, we'll get every .so file needed to run our Objective-C code in Android. In the next section, we'll see how to call it from the Java layer.

33.3 *Setting up the Java part*

The Java part will hold an Activity class and a TextFormatter class with the native method. The Activity is the following:

```
public class MainActivity extends Activity {
  private TextView mTextView;

  @Override
  public void onCreate(Bundle savedInstanceState) {
    super.onCreate(savedInstanceState);

    setContentView(R.layout.main);
    mTextView = (TextView) findViewById(R.id.text);
    String text = TextFormatter.formatString("Text from Java");    ◁——┘ Set a text to TextView using TextFormatter's formatString method
    mTextView.setText(text);
  }
}
```

The following is the TextFormatter Java code:

```
public class TextFormatter {
  public static native String formatString(String text);    ◁——┘ Native call declaration

  static {
    System.loadLibrary("macemu");    ◁——❶ Load all needed libraries
```

```
    System.loadLibrary("objc");
    System.loadLibrary("cf");
    System.loadLibrary("foundation");
    System.loadLibrary("textformatter");
    System.loadLibrary("main");
  }
}
```

The most important part of this piece of code is understanding what libraries will get loaded inside the static block ❶. They include the following:

- macemu: Contains emulation of some APIs used by objc4 and CoreFoundation libraries
- objc: objc4 runtime
- cf: CoreFoundation classes
- foundation: The Foundation library
- textformatter: Our TextFormatter library
- main: Our main library

When you run the application, you'll see a `TextView` populated with a mixture of texts from the Java and Objective-C worlds.

33.4   *The bottom line*

Using Itoa to port Objective-C applications to Android might be a good idea, depending on the type of code you need to port. I've used it to port business logic from iOS to Android and also to port cocos2d-iphone games to Android. My recommendation is that you give it a try and decide if it would work for you.

33.5   *External links*

www.nasatrainedmonkeys.com/portfolio/shaman-doctor/
www.cocos2d-iphone.org/
www.cocos2d-x.org/
www.itoaproject.com/
https://github.com/DmitrySkiba/itoa-ndk/wiki/Variables

Hack 34 *Using Scala inside Android*
Android v1.6+

If you've never heard of Scala, it's a multiparadigm programming language designed to integrate features of object-oriented programming and functional programming. Let's look at some of the benefits of using Scala, instead of Java, in Android to create a project:

- Less verbose than Java.
- It can use existing Java code.
- Closures.
- Dealing with threads is easier than in Java.

Discussing the benefits of Scala over Java is beyond the scope of this book, but let's look at what's possible with Scala. In this hack, we'll create a two-`Activity` application. One will be coded in Java and the other in Scala. This is a basic example we'll use to understand how to compile an Android application with Scala code.

As you might know, Android builds code by compiling your Java classes to byte-code, and afterward that bytecode is converted to dex. To make Scala code work inside Android, we need a tool that does all of this:

- Converts Scala code to bytecode
- Processes the Scala standard library to minimize the app size
- Processes Java code
- Creates an APK

Believe it or not, there are a lot of ways of getting this done. From my personal point of view, the best tool is SBT with its Android plugin.

What is *SBT*? SBT stands for *Simple Build Tool*. It's an open source build tool for Scala. Among its benefits:

- The project structure is similar to Maven.
- It manages dependencies using existing Maven and/or Ivy package repositories.
- It allows you to mix Scala and Java code.

What does the SBT Android plugin provide? The Android plugin is a script for creating a new Android project that SBT can compile. It also has several handy SBT targets for doing things such as packaging your app for the market and deploying to your device.

If we create a new Android application using the SBT Android plugin, we'll get a project directory structure similar to figure 34.1.

Since SBT allows Java code as well, we'll add our Java code inside src/main/java. Remember that, though Scala doesn't need to place files on a certain folder depending of the defined package, Java does. In this hack, we'll use

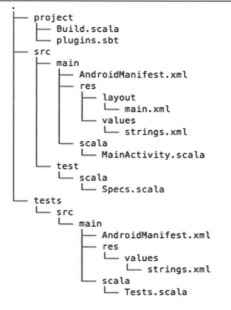

Figure 34.1   SBT Android plugin project structure

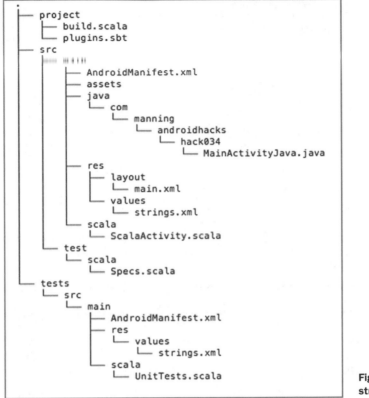

Figure 34.2 Project structure with Java code

com.manning .androidhacks.hack034 as our package, so we need to create a directory structure that respects that. The correct project structure for adding a second Java `Activity` can be seen in figure 34.2.

Let's look at the `Activity` done in Java and how it connects to the Scala `Activity`. Here's the code:

```java
public class MainActivityJava extends Activity {

  @Override
  public void onCreate(Bundle savedInstanceState) {
    super.onCreate(savedInstanceState);
    setContentView(R.layout.main);
  }

  public void buttonClick(View v) {
    startActivity(new Intent(this, ScalaActivity.class));    ❶
  }
}
```

❶ **Start Activity coded in Scala**

Do we need to do anything different to call the `Activity` done in Scala? No, there isn't anything special. We start the Scala `Activity` as any ordinary `Activity` ❶.

Now let's take a look at the Scala `Activity` code to see what's there:

```
class ScalaActivity extends Activity {
  override def onCreate(savedInstanceState: Bundle) {
    super.onCreate(savedInstanceState)
    setContentView(new TextView(this) {
      setText("Activity coded in Scala ")
    })
  }
}
```

❶ **Anonymous subclass of TextView is set as content view**

You can see that the Scala `Activity`'s code is 100% Scala. The Scala coded there comes from the demo application created by the SBT Android plugin. Take a closer look at how the content view is set ❶. That line creates an anonymous subclass of the `TextView`, and with the help of an initializer block it calls the `setText()` method.

To run the application, we can launch SBT and execute the following:

- `android:package-debug`
- `android:start-device`

Unfortunately, creating an APK takes a while. This two-`Activity` application takes me about one full minute to compile. You should know that this isn't Scala's fault. What takes so long is the ProGuard pass that goes through the Scala library and removes any unused part of it. To solve this issue, some developers add the Scala libraries to their developing device. There's even an Android application that installs Scala on your device if it's rooted.

34.1   *The bottom line*

Scala is gaining a lot of momentum in the Java world, and it's also attracting interest in the community of Android developers. Learning a new language might feel time-consuming, but Scala is something that every Java developer should try.

34.2   *External links*

http://www.scala-lang.org/
http://en.wikipedia.org/wiki/Simple_Build_Tool
https://github.com/jberkel/android-plugin
http://nevercertain.com/2011/02/03/scala-android-intellij-win-part-1-prerequisites.html
https://github.com/scala-android-libs/scala-android-libs

Ready-to-use snippets

Do you sometimes use the same code in different applications? If so, this chapter is for you. We'll go through some code snippets that you can copy and paste into any Android application.

Hack 35 *Firing up multiple intents*
Android v2.1+

One of the nicest features about Android is the `intent` system. If you want to share something with another application, you can use an `intent` to do so. If you want to open a link, you have an `intent` for that. In Android, almost everything can be done with an `intent`.

If you use the mobile messenger app, WhatsApp, you might know that you can share images with your contacts from an image in the gallery or by taking a photo. The dialog presented to the user to pick an image from the gallery or to take a picture is shown in figure 35.1. Obviously, this was created with `intents` but, unfortunately, it can't be done with only one.

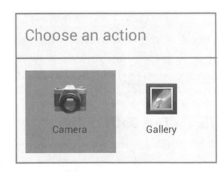

Figure 35.1   Dialog to choose how to handle an action

117

In this hack, we'll analyze how this can be done. We'll see which is the `intent` to take a photo, which is the `intent` to pick a picture from the gallery, and how to combine both.

35.1 *Taking a picture*

The `intent` to take a photo using the camera app is the following:

```
Intent takePhotoIntent = new Intent(MediaStore.ACTION_IMAGE_CAPTURE);
Intent chooserIntent = Intent.createChooser(takePhotoIntent,
  getString(R.string.activity_main_pick_picture));
startActivityForResult(chooserIntent, TAKE_PICTURE);
```

35.2 *Picking a picture from the gallery*

To pick an image from the gallery, we do this:

```
Intent pickIntent = new Intent(Intent.ACTION_GET_CONTENT);
pickIntent.setType("image/*");
Intent chooserIntent = Intent.createChooser(pickIntent,
  getString(R.string.activity_main_take_picture));
startActivityForResult(chooserIntent, PICK_PICTURE);
```

35.3 *Mixing both intents*

Since Android API level 5, we can create a chooser and add extra initial `intents`. This means that instead of using just one type of `intent`, we can use several. An example of usage:

```
Intent pickIntent = new Intent(Intent.ACTION_GET_CONTENT);      ◁─┐ Create pick
 pickIntent.setType("image/*");                                    │ image intent

Intent takePhotoIntent;
takePhotoIntent = new Intent(MediaStore.ACTION_IMAGE_CAPTURE);

Intent chooserIntent = Intent.createChooser(pickIntent,         Add take photo
    getString(R.string.activity_main_pick_both));               intent as an extra
chooserIntent.putExtra(Intent.EXTRA_INITIAL_INTENTS,         ◁─┘ initial intent
    new Intent[]{takePhotoIntent});

startActivityForResult(chooserIntent, PICK_OR_TAKE_PICTURE);
```

Create take photo intent → (points to `takePhotoIntent = new Intent(MediaStore.ACTION_IMAGE_CAPTURE);`)

Using the previous code will show all applications that handle both `intents`, taking a photo and picking a picture. Remember that we need to override the `onActivity-Result()` method inside our `Activity` to do something with the image picked/taken by the user.

35.4 *The bottom line*

It's important that you understand how `intents` work. It's a key part of the Android environment and using them correctly will make your app work well with other apps. For example, if your app uses the code shown here and inside the device there's a file browser application, it's likely that the apps will work together to provide the best experience for the user.

35.5 *External links*

www.whatsapp.com/

http://stackoverflow.com/questions/11021021/
    how-to-make-an-intent-with-multiple-actions

http://stackoverflow.com/questions/2708128/
    single-intent-to-let-user-take-picture-or-pick-image-from-gallery-in-android

Hack 36 *Getting user information when receiving feedback*
Android v1.6+

Listening to your users' feedback is one of many ways to help make your application successful. User feedback can highlight which sections they enjoy the most, and they'll likely ask for new features that help to improve your application. During my years as a developer in the Android market, I've noticed that every time I fix a bug or add a feature requested by a user, more people start downloading my application. What's at play here is word of mouth. The preceding is a good scenario—users let the developer know what problem they're having, though sometimes users don't provide enough explanation, which makes it difficult to identify the problem.

In this hack, I'll show you how to append users' device information to their feedback emails. This means it'll be easier to learn important details from your users and get their problems fixed as soon as possible.

Figure 36.1   Feedback email

You can see the finished feature in figure 36.1. From the information provided, you can glean that I'm running the application version 1.0 from a Nexus One and that I'm in Argentina using an English locale.

To create this, we'll use two classes—one that takes care of collecting all of the information, and one that takes care of preparing the `intent` to send the email with feedback. Let's first look at `EnvironmentInfoUtil.java`:

```
public class EnvironmentInfoUtil {

  public static String getApplicationInfo(Context context) {
    return String.format("%s\n%s\n%s\n%s\n%s\n%s\n",
```

Convenience method to get all available information

```
            getCountry(context), getBrandInfo(), getModelInfo(),
            getDeviceInfo(), getVersionInfo(context),
            getLocale(context));
    }
    public static String getCountry(Context context) {
        TelephonyManager mTelephonyMgr = (TelephonyManager) context
            .getSystemService(Context.TELEPHONY_SERVICE);
        return String.format("Country: %s", mTelephonyMgr
            .getNetworkCountryIso());
    }
    public static String getModelInfo() {
        return String.format("Model: %s", Build.MODEL);
    }

    ...

    public static String getLocale(Context context) {
        return String.format("Locale: %s", context.getResources()
            .getConfiguration().locale.getDisplayName());
    }

    ...

}
```

TelephonyManager is used to identify country user is in

Getting info from Build class

Context is used to get user's locale

We already have a class that takes care of getting the information, but how do we send that through an email? We use the LaunchEmailUtil class:

```
public class LaunchEmailUtil {

    public static void launchEmailToIntent(Context context) {
        Intent msg = new Intent(Intent.ACTION_SEND);

        StringBuilder body = new StringBuilder("\n\n----------\n");
        body.append(EnvironmentInfoUtil.getApplicationInfo(context));

        msg.putExtra(Intent.EXTRA_EMAIL,
            context.getString(R.string.mail_support_feedback_to)
                .split(", "));
        msg.putExtra(Intent.EXTRA_SUBJECT,
            context.getString(R.string.mail_support_feedback_subject));
        msg.putExtra(Intent.EXTRA_TEXT, body.toString());

        msg.setType("message/rfc822");

        context.startActivity(Intent.createChooser(msg,
            context.getString(R.string.pref_sendemail_title)));
    }
}
```

Method to be called from the Activity ❶

❷ Setting recipient

Setting body text using Environment-InfoUtil's information ❸

Setting title for the picker ❹

We can use this class from an Activity using the launchEmailToIntent() method ❶. The logic is simple: we identify to whom we should send the email from strings.xml ❷, and we provide a subject ❸. Just in case the user has more than one application that takes care of sending emails, we'll create a picker with a custom title ❹.

36.1 The bottom line

Being responsive to user feedback is a good way to improve your application's popularity. Always remember to tell your users when you're going to send private information.

36.2 External links

http://developer.android.com/reference/android/os/Build.html

http://developer.android.com/reference/android/telephony/TelephonyManager.html

Hack 37 *Adding an MP3 to the media ContentProvider*
Android v1.6+

If you're an Android user, you should know that whenever you want to listen to new music on your device, the only thing you need to do is copy those files onto the external storage (usually an SD card). After the files are copied, you can open your music player and the files will be there. How does this work?

Inside Android is something called a ContentProvider. A ContentProvider is the correct way to offer data to external applications. For example, Android has a contacts ContentProvider. This means that inside your device is an application (Contacts) that offers a ContentProvider to handle contacts. As you can imagine, you'll also find a media ContentProvider.

When you copy your media files to the external storage, there's a process that will browse all the folders looking for media, and it will add it to the media Content-Provider. After media's added to the ContentProvider, everyone can use it.

Imagine you're creating an application that downloads music. It's important that every media file you download gets added to the media ContentProvider. Otherwise, the user will not be able to use that media from another application.

In this hack, we'll look at two possible ways to add an MP3 file to the media Content-Provider. The demo application will hold two MP3 files in the res/raw folder and we'll copy them to the external storage. After they're copied, we can let the Content-Provider know that we've added new media.

37.1 Adding the MP3 using content values

As with any other ContentProvider, we can add items to it using ContentValues. The code is the following:

```
MediaUtils.saveRaw(this, R.raw.loop1, LOOP1_PATH);

ContentValues values = new ContentValues(5);
```

◁─── **File is first saved in external storage**

```
values.put(Media.ARTIST, "Android");
values.put(Media.ALBUM, "60AH");
values.put(Media.TITLE, "hack037");
values.put(Media.MIME_TYPE, "audio/mp3");
values.put(Media.DATA, LOOP1_PATH);

getContentResolver().insert(
  Media.EXTERNAL_CONTENT_URI, values);
```

◁— **Complete all necessary fields to insert media**

◁— **Insert values to Content-Provider using its URI**

37.2 *Adding the MP3 using the media scanner*

The code included in the last section works fine, but it has a big problem. Some values were set by hand and perhaps it would be better to read them from the file. For example, the real author of loop1.mp3 is "calpomatt" and not "Android." We'd know that by reading the MP3's metadata.

Fortunately, there's a way to avoid having to add those values by hand. The code is the following:

```
MediaUtils.saveRaw(this, R.raw.loop2, LOOP2_PATH);
```
◁— **File is first saved in external storage**

```
Uri uri = Uri.parse("file://" + LOOP2_PATH);
Intent i = new Intent(Intent.ACTION_MEDIA_SCANNER_SCAN_FILE, uri);
sendBroadcast(i);
```
◁— **Send a broadcast asking for a particular file to be scanned and added**

37.3 *The bottom line*

If you're creating an application that handles media, you should pay attention to the media ContentProvider. Try understanding and using it correctly. It might be essential to your users.

37.4 *External links*

http://developer.android.com/guide/topics/providers/content-providers.html
http://stackoverflow.com/questions/3735771/adding-mp3-to-the-contentresolver
www.flashkit.com/loops/Pop-Rock/Rock/Get_P-calpomat-4517/index.php
www.flashkit.com/loops/Pop-Rock/Rock/_Hard-XtremeWe-6500/index.php

Hack 38 Adding a refresh action to the action bar
Android v2.1+

The ActionBar API was added to Android version 3.0 (Honeycomb). The idea behind the ActionBar pattern is to have a place where you locate the user inside your application and offer contextual actions.

You might have noticed that some applications have a refresh action in their ActionBars. You see a Refresh icon and when you press it, a refresh process runs while a ProgressBar spins. Unfortunately, the platform doesn't contain a widget—it needs to be created by hand. In this hack, I'll show you how to do it.

For the sake of compatibility we'll use Jake Wharton's ActionBarSherlock library. ActionBarSherlock offers the ActionBar API, but it can be used in older Android versions.

> **ABOUT ACTIONBARSHERLOCK** You'll need to know how to configure your application to use ActionBarSherlock to move on. You can learn how by visiting the library's web page: http://actionbarsherlock.com/.

Figure 38.1 Basic ActionBar

To add an ActionBar to an Activity, the first step is to make our application use the ActionBarSherlock theme. We can do this by using the following lines in the AndroidManifest.xml file:

```
<application
    android:icon="@drawable/ic_launcher"
    android:label="@string/app_name"
    android:theme="@style/Theme.Sherlock">
```

The second step is to create an activity, but instead of extending Activity, we need to extend SherlockActivity. The code to show a progress icon in the action bar is the following:

```
public class MainActivity extends SherlockActivity {
  private static final int MENU_REFRESH = 10;
  private MenuItem mRefreshMenu;

  ...

  @Override
  public boolean onCreateOptionsMenu(Menu menu) {              Create
    mRefreshMenu = menu.add(MENU_REFRESH, MENU_REFRESH,        refresh
      MENU_REFRESH, "Refresh");                          ◁     menu
    mRefreshMenu.setIcon(R.drawable.menu_reload);
    mRefreshMenu.setShowAsAction(MenuItem.SHOW_AS_ACTION_ALWAYS);

    return true;
  }
}
```

The result can be seen in figure 38.1.

The next step is to handle what to do when a user presses the Refresh button in the action bar or the button in the middle of the screen. Both items should launch a background task. To simulate the background task, we'll create an AsyncTask with the following code:

```
private class LoadingAsyncTask extends AsyncTask<Void, Void, Void> {

  @Override
  protected void onPreExecute() {           Handle UI changes
    super.onPreExecute();                   when the  task is
    startLoading();                         about to start
  }

  @Override
  protected Void doInBackground(Void... params) {    Sleep for
    SystemClock.sleep(5000L);                        5 seconds
    return null;
  }

  @Override
  protected void onPostExecute(Void result) {    Handle UI changes
    super.onPostExecute(result);                 when the task is
    stopLoading();                               about to finish
  }
}
```

The execution of the AsyncTask is accomplished by a single method:

```
public void handleRefresh(View v) {
  new LoadingAsyncTask().execute();
}
```

This method is called from the centered button from the Activity's layout using the android:onClick property and from the action bar in the onOptionsItemSelected() method.

We have almost everything in place. The only missing part is how to handle UI changes when the background process starts and finishes. For the centered button, the logic is simple. We want to disable the button while the background task is working and enable it when finished. We can do this by using the setEnabled(boolean enabled) method. The big question here is how to replace the progress menu item with something spinning. To do that, we'll use an ActionView.

The ActionView is explained in the documentation (see section 38.2):

An action view is a widget that appears in the action bar as a substitute for an action item's button. For example, if you have an item in the options menu for "Search," you can add an action view that replaces the button with a SearchView widget, as shown in figure [38.2].

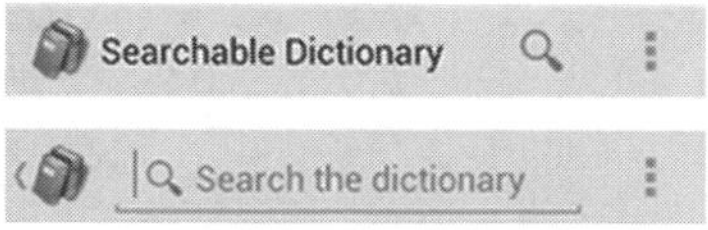

Figure 38.2   An action bar with a collapsed ActionView for Search (top) and an expanded ActionView with the SearchView widget (bottom)

Because we'll add the spinning widget through an ActionView, let's create the view with XML:

```xml
<?xml version="1.0" encoding="utf-8"?>
<LinearLayout xmlns:android="http://schemas.android.com/apk/res/android"
    style="?attr/actionButtonStyle"
    android:layout_width="wrap_content"
    android:layout_height="wrap_content"
    android:addStatesFromChildren="true"
    android:focusable="true"
    android:gravity="center"
    android:paddingLeft="4dp"
    android:paddingRight="4dp" >

    <ProgressBar
        android:layout_width="30dp"
        android:layout_height="30dp"
        android:focusable="true" />

</LinearLayout>
```

Now that we have the XML, the rest is quite simple. This is how the startLoading() and stopLoading() methods handle the refresh menu item's action view:

```java
private void startLoading() {
  mRefreshMenu.setActionView(R.layout.menu_item_refresh);
  mButton.setEnabled(false);
}
private void stopLoading() {
  mRefreshMenu.setActionView(null);
  mButton.setEnabled(true);
}
```

38.1 *The bottom line*

This hack is an example of how to customize the action bar's items. Nowadays, using an action bar is almost a must for every Android application, and thanks to Jake Wharton we have an Android library that backports the action bar to older platforms. It's important to learn what's possible and understand how it can fulfill your application use cases.

38.2 *External links*

http://developer.android.com/guide/topics/ui/actionbar.html
http://actionbarsherlock.com/

Hack 39 *Getting dependencies from the market*
Android v1.6+

It's common in Android to find applications that use other applications to help perform tasks. Thanks to Android's `Intent` system, you can ask other applications to help you finish a task. For example, instead of adding the logic to take a photo using the camera, you can ask the photo application to do it for you and return the result. Because you can create a program that offers its functionalities through an `intent` call, the market has lots of applications your application can use.

In this hack, we'll see how to check if an application is installed before trying to launch an `intent` call. If it's not installed, we'll ask the user to get it from the market. For this example, we'll use Layar. Layar is an application that offers a mobile browser that allows users to find various items based upon augmented reality technology. Developers can create something called a *layer*, which shows points of interest inside Layar's browser. We'll create an ordinary Android program that will have a link to a Layar's layer. To create our application we'll need the following:

- A way to know if Layar is installed
- Code to open the market to download Layar
- The `intent` call to open a specific layer

To check if Layar is installed, we'll use the `PackageManager` class. The code to make this check is the following:

```
public static boolean isLayarAvailable(Context ctx) {
  PackageManager pm = ctx.getPackageManager();

  try {

    pm.getApplicationInfo("com.layar", 0);          ◁┘ PackageManager's
    return true;                                        getApplicationInfo()
                                                        method
  } catch (PackageManager.NameNotFoundException e) {
                                                     ◁┘ Indicates
    return false;                                       application
  }                                                      isn't available

}
```

The easiest way to check if an application is available is to use `PackageManager`'s `getApplicationInfo()` method, using the application's package name. If it exists, it'll return an instance of `ApplicationInfo` populated with information collected from the AndroidManifest.xml's `<application>` tag. If, while trying to get the application information, we get a `NameNotFoundException`, we can be sure that the application isn't available.

Now let's run the code to open the market:

```
public static AlertDialog showDownloadDialog(final Context ctx) {

  AlertDialog.Builder downloadDialog = new AlertDialog.Builder(ctx);
```

```
downloadDialog.setTitle("Layar is not available");
downloadDialog
    .setMessage("Do you want to download it from the market?");
downloadDialog.setPositiveButton("Yes",
    new DialogInterface.OnClickListener() {

        @Override
        public void onClick(DialogInterface dialogInterface, int i) {
            Uri uri = Uri.parse("market://details?id=com.layar");
            Intent intent = new Intent(Intent.ACTION_VIEW, uri);
            try {
                ctx.startActivity(intent);
            } catch (ActivityNotFoundException e) {
                Toast.makeText(ctx, "Market not installed",
                    Toast.LENGTH_SHORT).show();
            }
        }

    });

downloadDialog.setNegativeButton("No",
    new DialogInterface.OnClickListener() {

        @Override
        public void onClick(DialogInterface dialogInterface, int i) {
        }

    });

return downloadDialog.show();
}
```

> Create an AlertDialog to let users decide if they want to download Layar from the market.

> To launch the market, we can use the uri scheme in conjunction with Intent's **ACTION_VIEW** action.

> Some Android-powered devices might not have the market application. This try-catch will ensure the application won't crash.

> After creating the AlertDialog, we can show it.

The final step is to add the login so we can decide if we should download Layar or launch our layer through an `intent`. This is the logic executed when a button is clicked:

```
public void onLayarClick(View v) {
    if ( !ActivityHelper.isLayarAvailable(this) ) {

        ActivityHelper.showDownloadDialog(this);

    } else {

        Intent intent = new Intent();
        intent.setAction(Intent.ACTION_VIEW);
        Uri uri = Uri.parse("layar://teather/?action=refresh");
        intent.setData(uri);
        startActivity(intent);

    }

}
```

> Logic to show the download dialog.

> If Layar is available, use its uri scheme to show the teather layer inside the Layar application.

39.1 The bottom line

A lot of applications are available that offer these kinds of `intent` APIs. Using them provides two important benefits. The first one is obvious: you'll code less. The second is that your users might already be using the second application. This means they won't need to learn a second way of doing things. For example, if you want your program to grab snapshots, instead of providing a new way to do it, you can ask it to use the photo application, which is well known by every Android user.

39.2 *External links*

http://layar.com/

http://developer.android.com/reference/android/content/pm/PackageManager.html

http://developer.android.com/reference/android/app/AlertDialog.html

Hack 40 *Last-in-first-out image loading*
Android v2.1+
Contributed by William Sanville

One challenge that developers commonly face is displaying images from a network location. This challenge often comes in different forms, such as displaying many images in a list. An ideal solution for this type of challenge will include

- Maintaining a responsive UI
- Performing network and disk I/O outside the application's UI thread
- Support for view recycling, as in the case of a `ListView`
- A caching mechanism for quickly displaying images

Many solutions to this problem use an in-memory cache for holding previously loaded images and a thread pool for queuing up images to load. But an often-overlooked feature is the order in which images are requested.

Consider the case of a `ListView` where each row contains an image. If a user "flings" the list in the downward direction, most image-loading solutions will request each image in the order its parent `View` is displayed on the screen. As a result, when the user stops scrolling, the rows currently on the screen, which are the most important rows at the current point in time, will load last. What you want is for the last-requested rows to "jump the queue" and be processed first.

40.1 *Starting point: Android sample application*

The Android Training section of the official documentation includes the article (see section 40.6) "Displaying Bitmaps Efficiently," which we'll use as our starting point. The article covers core concepts such as downsampling images to the proper size, using the `LruCache` class for in-memory caching (available in the Support Library, version 4), and a basic mechanism for performing work off the UI thread.

We'll expand on this example application to meet the goal of loading the most recently requested images first. We'll also make performance improvements over the original version by removing the problematic use of one AsyncTask instance per get-View() call by the application's adapter. The sample implementation makes it possible to cause a runtime exception when scrolling up and down several times, resulting in a RejectedExecutionException caused by too many AsyncTask instances, so that's fixed in the final example.

40.2 Introducing executors

The AsyncTask solution isn't suitable for large number of images, nor will it give us control over the priority of our tasks. Instead, we'll use an executor service from the java.util.concurrent package and a priority queue to specify the order in which we request images. With the new implementation, we can maintain methods similar to AsyncTask, namely, cancelling tasks which have been pushed offscreen. Our last-in-first-out (LIFO) implementation will involve two classes, LIFOTask and LIFO-ThreadPoolProcessor.

Our new task object will maintain a static variable indicating the number of instances created. This will serve as the priority for the task, because a newly created task will have a higher counter. We use this counter to implement a compareTo() method, for sorting purposes later:

```
public class LIFOTask extends FutureTask<Object>
  implements Comparable<LIFOTask> {

  private static long counter = 0;
  private final long priority;

  public LIFOTask(Runnable runnable) {
    super(runnable, new Object());
    priority = counter++;            ◁─┐ Tasks in this example
  }                                       are all created on the
  public long getPriority() {             same thread.
    return priority;
  }

  @Override
  public int compareTo(LIFOTask other) {
    return priority > other.getPriority() ? -1 : 1;
  }
}
```

Our choice of base class here is important. We extend FutureTask, a class accepted by the executor classes because it exposes a cancel method, much like the old implementation using AsyncTask.

Building off the LIFOTask class, we'll use its compareTo() method and the Thread-PoolExecutor class:

```
public class LIFOThreadPoolProcessor {
  private BlockingQueue<Runnable> opsToRun =
  new PriorityBlockingQueue<Runnable>(64, new Comparator<Runnable>() {
    @Override
    public int compare(Runnable r0, Runnable r1) {
```

```
      if (r0 instanceof LIFOTask && r1 instanceof LIFOTask) {
        LIFOTask l0 = (LIFOTask)r0;
        LIFOTask l1 = (LIFOTask)r1;
        return l0.compareTo(l1);
      }

      return 0;
    }
  });

  private ThreadPoolExecutor executor;

  public LIFOThreadPoolProcessor(int threadCount) {
    executor = new ThreadPoolExecutor(threadCount, threadCount, 0,
      TimeUnit.SECONDS, opsToRun);
  }

  public Future<?> submitTask(LIFOTask task) {
    return executor.submit(task);
  }

  public void clear() {
    executor.purge();
  }
}
```

The noteworthy part of the class is the parameters passed to the `ThreadPoolExecutor` constructor. We let the client application choose the exact thread pool size, and choose a `PriorityBlockingQueue` to hold the incoming tasks that the client application submits. We then use the `compareTo()` method of the `LIFOTask` object to get our desired ordering. Note that in this case, the `keepAlive` parameter is not applicable given the core and max thread pool sizes used.

40.3   *UI thread—leaving and returning seamlessly*

As Android developers, we know the importance of maintaining a responsive UI, so we offload time-consuming tasks, like I/O, to a background thread. Often, when this work is done, we want to update the UI. Android, much like other UI systems you may be familiar with, isn't thread-safe. We must return to the main application thread before modifying any `ImageView`s. Attempting to modify the UI from outside the main thread will cause an exception.

The original implementation used the `onPostExecute()` method of `AsyncTask`. Because we're replacing the use of `AsyncTask` with an executor, we'll instead give a `Runnable` to our host activity. We'll use the `runOnUiThread()` method of the `Activity` class, which will use a `Handler` under the hood to get our work added to the UI's message queue.

Slipping something into the UI thread doesn't come free of consideration. We have to be mindful of the following:

- `ImageView` instances may be recycled if a user scrolls in a `ListView`.
- The host activity may be destroyed before a task finishes.

As a result, every step of the `Runnable` used to process images checks if it should stop performing work. A stop condition is detected if the host activity sets a flag with `ImageWorker`'s `setExitTasksEarly()` method, which should be called from `onPause()`. Additionally, a stop condition is detected if the `cancel()` method of `FutureTask` is called.

40.4 Considerations

For use in a production application, the Android Training article suggests using a better disk-caching solution. The implementation provided in the original article is lacking in a few key areas. To provide a more complete example here, the disk cache implementation was modified to support rebuilding the disk cache upon application restarts, and no longer maintains two copies of downloaded files.

40.5 The bottom line

Time-consuming work, such as loading images, needs to be performed outside the UI thread. This will allow built-in components, such as `ListView`, to operate smoothly. You can give users a better experience by fine-tuning the order in which you load images using a LIFO queue.

Using a potentially unbounded number of `AsyncTask` instances is problematic, and the job can be better fulfilled by using executors. Additionally, Android provides a solid implementation of `LruCache` in the support library for implementing efficient caching solutions.

40.6 External links

http://developer.android.com/training/displaying-bitmaps/index.html
http://developer.android.com/tools/extras/support-library.html#Using
http://developer.android.com/reference/java/util/concurrent/ExecutorService.html
http://developer.android.com/reference/java/util/concurrent/FutureTask.html

Beyond database basics

If you've been developing Android applications, you may have used a database to persist information. In this chapter, we'll cover some advanced tips for developers who are familiar with using databases in Android.

Hack 41 *Building databases with ORMLite*

Android v2.2+
Contributed by William Sanville

Android applications usually have a requirement for some form of persistent storage, meaning data that's saved between each time a user runs the application. To facilitate this need, Android ships with a relational database called SQLite. This hack covers creating an entire database instance using a tool called ORMLite, an Object-Relational Mapping (ORM) tool, as well as reading and writing data.

Our end goal is to create an application that displays articles broken down in categories and allows users to comment on each article. The finished application can be seen in figure 41.1.

Figure 41.1 Finished application

All database operations in this application are performed using ORMLite, rather than writing any SQL statements by hand. This approach can save time by reducing the amount of code needed to create the database schema.

41.1   *A simple data model*

The end result will have a list of categories and subcategories, with article titles. Clicking an article will bring the user to a new activity, which will display more article information, as well as allow the user to create comments. Graphically, our application will use the data model illustrated in figure 41.2.

The diagram describes a database that allows the following:

- A Category has an ID and a title. It can also have one parent Category, but that isn't required, because topmost categories won't have a parent.
- An Article has an ID, title, body text, and a date indicating when it was created.
- An Author has an ID, name, and email address.
- Articles can belong to many different categories, and categories can have many articles.
- Articles can be written by multiple authors, and authors can write many articles.
- A Comment is about a single article and contains an ID, the name of the user who added the comment, some text, and a date indicating when it was created.
- Articles can have many comments.

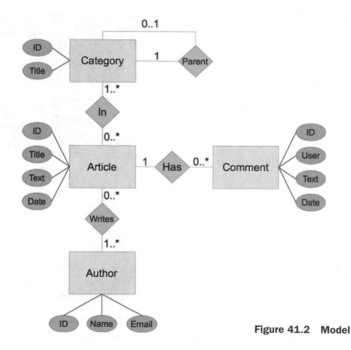

Figure 41.2   Model

When designing an application that needs a relational database, it's useful to first start with a diagram of the data model like this one. This is known as an entity-relationship diagram (ER diagram). ER diagrams are used during the design stage of development to identify different entities and the relationships between them.

41.2 Getting started

ORMLite requires two JAR files from the releases section: core and android. This application uses version 4.41. After obtaining the dependencies, we'll start creating our database schema.

The first step to using ORMLite is to implement the actual Java classes we'll work with in our application. During this process, we'll take special care to include annotations on our classes that will allow ORMLite to create the needed tables. This will also provide the ORM tool with information about how it should behave when querying the database for our objects, in the case of complex relations. Note that the annotations approach is one of several ways to specify the database schema generated by ORMLite.

The two most common annotations we'll use with ORMLite are `DatabaseTable` and `DatabaseField`. These annotations will target classes and member variables respectively and will allow us to craft our resulting database tables. A simple implementation of the `Article` class might look like the following using annotations:

```
@DatabaseTable
public class Article {
  @DatabaseField(generatedId = true)
  public int id;

  @DatabaseField
  public String title, text;

  @DatabaseField
  public Date publishedDate;           ORMLite requires
                                       parameterless
  public Article() {              <──┘ constructor
  }
}
```

This class, when part of a full implementation, would result in the following CREATE TABLE SQL statement:

```
CREATE TABLE 'article'
  ('title' VARCHAR, 'publishedDate' VARCHAR, 'text' VARCHAR,
  'id' INTEGER PRIMARY KEY AUTOINCREMENT);
```

Note the annotation on the field `id`. We specify the parameter `generatedId = true` to signify that this field is our primary key, and it should be automatically assigned by SQLite. Also note that, by default, ORMLite uses our class name as the SQL table and the names of the member variables as the columns of the table.

Last, observe that ORMLite requires a zero-parameter constructor on the classes it operates on. When ORMLite creates an instance of this class, in the case of a query which returns articles, it will use the parameterless constructor and set member variables using reflection (ORMLite can also use setters for member variables if preferred).

41.3 *Rock-solid database schema*

Building upon the first and simplest example of crafting a table from a Java class, we'll demonstrate the following:

- Custom names for tables and columns
- Handling relationships between classes
- Referential integrity for relationships (API Level 8 and above)
- Cascading deletes (API Level 8 and above)
- Uniqueness constraints for cross references

Most real-world database instances will use these concepts and others. Even though we're using an ORM tool to build our tables, we still have the expressive power to achieve a solid schema to enforce data consistency. For example, we might want to require that an article's title and text must not be null. We also can ensure that if a category has a parent category, the parent must actually exist. Furthermore, we can specify that if an article is deleted, then all of its comments and mappings to categories will be deleted automatically by SQLite.

The first recommendation when defining our schema is to use final variables to define names for tables and columns. This, in practice, will make maintaining our code much easier in the scenario where a member variable is refactored or removed. Doing so will help cause compile-time errors, rather than tricky-to-spot runtime mistakes hidden away in SQL strings. Let's define the `Category` class using this technique. We'll declare public static final variables for the table and columns:

```java
@DatabaseTable(tableName = Category.TABLE_NAME)        ◁  Specifies name ❶
public class Category {                                    of our table
  public static final String TABLE_NAME = "categories",
      ID_COLUMN = "_id",
      NAME_COLUMN = "name",
      PARENT_COLUMN = "parent";

  @DatabaseField(generatedId = true, columnName = ID_COLUMN)    ❸ Name
  private int id;                                                 member
                                                                  must not
  @DatabaseField(canBeNull = false, columnName = NAME_COLUMN)  ◁ be null
  private String name;

  @DatabaseField(foreign = true, columnName = PARENT_COLUMN)   ◁  Marked as
  private Category parent;                                     ❹ foreign

  public Category() {
  }
}
```

Specifies names of columns in the DatabaseField ❷

The additions here are many, and we're not done yet. We now specify the name of our table in the `DatabaseTable` ❶ annotation and names of columns in the `Database-Field` ❷ annotations. We can use these public variables elsewhere in the host application for querying purposes.

Additionally, we require that the name member must not be null (columns can be null by default) ❸. Finally, consider the annotation on the parent member. Any member variable which is defined as a table in our relation must be marked as foreign, using `foreign = true` ❹. This instructs ORMLite to only store the ID of the foreign object in the current table. Taking this class one step further, we can ensure that a parent category must exist. The final member declaration of the parent looks like the following:

```
@DatabaseField(foreign = true, foreignAutoRefresh = true,
  columnName = PARENT_COLUMN, columnDefinition = "integer references " +
  TABLE_NAME + "(" + ID_COLUMN + ") on delete cascade")
private Category parent;
```

We can fine-tune the exact SQL used to define this column using `columnDefinition`. Here we have specified that the parent column has a foreign key to the categories table (the same table on which it is defined). This states that values in the parent column must either be null or exist in the categories table in the _id column. We also specify that records that refer to a parent category get deleted when the parent category is deleted. This is known as a *cascading delete*. This last technique is not required in a database, but for demonstration purposes we'll include it. Our finished table for the `Category` class looks like the following:

```
CREATE TABLE 'categories' ('parent' integer references categories(_id)
  on delete cascade, 'name' VARCHAR NOT NULL ,
  '_id' INTEGER PRIMARY KEY AUTOINCREMENT )
```

The last concept in this section is specifying uniqueness in a column or combination of columns. Implementing the many-to-many relationship between articles and categories requires a cross-reference table. Put simply, a cross-reference table is used to match up entries from one table with entries from another. Therefore, we'll define a two-column table to match IDs from articles to IDs from categories, logically storing which articles are in which categories. As an added sanity check, cross-reference tables usually include a constraint saying that the same combination of IDs can only appear in the table once. To express uniqueness, ORMLite uses two Boolean elements, `unique` and `uniqueCombo`. We'll set `uniqueCombo = true` on the two member variables in the following class, `ArticleCategory`, which maps articles to categories:

```
@DatabaseTable(tableName = ArticleCategory.TABLE_NAME)
public class ArticleCategory {
  public static final String TABLE_NAME = "articlecategories",     ◄─❶
      ARTICLE_ID_COLUMN = "article_id",
      CATEGORY_ID_COLUMN = "category_id";

  @DatabaseField(foreign = true, canBeNull = false, uniqueCombo = true,
      columnName = ARTICLE_ID_COLUMN,
      columnDefinition = "integer references " +           ◄─
      Article.TABLE_NAME +
      "(" + Article.ID_COLUMN + ") on delete cascade")      ❷
  private Article article;

  @DatabaseField(foreign = true, canBeNull = false,
      uniqueCombo = true,                                   ◄─
      columnName = CATEGORY_ID_COLUMN,
```

❶ **Final variables for table and column names**

❷ **Using the columnDefinition element**

❸ **Setting foreign = true for storing complex objects**

```
      columnDefinition = "integer references " +
      Category.TABLE_NAME +
      "(" + Category.ID_COLUMN + ") on delete cascade")
  private Category category;

  public ArticleCategory() {
  }
}
```

Notice the use of techniques described earlier, such as final variables for table and column names ❶, referential integrity using the columnDefinition element ❷, and the requirement of setting foreign = true ❸ when storing complex objects. The resulting table is as follows:

```
CREATE TABLE 'articlecategories'
  ('article_id' integer references articles(_id) on delete cascade,
  'category_id' integer references categories(_id) on delete cascade,
  UNIQUE ('article_id','category_id') );
```

Note the UNIQUE statement in the generated SQL.

41.4   *SQLiteOpenHelper—your gateway to the database*

SQLiteOpenHelper is an abstract class provided with Android that's used to manage the interaction between the developer and the database file stored on a device. Developers are tasked with subclassing SQLiteOpenHelper and implementing two methods: onCreate() and onUpgrade(). The onCreate() method is where a developer specifies the exact schema of the database, and onUpgrade() is used in subsequent releases if a schema change is needed.

When using ORMLite, instead of extending SQLiteOpenHelper, we'll instead extend OrmLiteSqliteOpenHelper to gain the benefits of using an ORM tool. We still, however, are tasked with implementing the onCreate() and onUpgrade() methods. Fortunately, all of the work done when carefully declaring the annotations on our classes makes this extremely easy. We'll use static methods on the TableUtils class to create all of our needed tables. Under the hood, ORMLite will use Java's reflection APIs to read our annotations and build the create table SQL statements we saw earlier.

Now that the hard work is already done, our implementation of the onCreate() method is the following:

```
@Override
public void onCreate(SQLiteDatabase sqLiteDatabase,
    ConnectionSource connectionSource) {
  try {
    TableUtils.createTable(connectionSource, Category.class);
    TableUtils.createTable(connectionSource, Article.class);
    TableUtils.createTable(connectionSource, ArticleCategory.class);
    TableUtils.createTable(connectionSource, Author.class);
    TableUtils.createTable(connectionSource, ArticleAuthor.class);
    TableUtils.createTable(connectionSource, Comment.class);
  } catch (SQLException e) {
    Log.e(TAG, "Unable to create tables.", e);
```

```
      throw new RuntimeException(e);
    }
  }
}
```

Note that when using foreign keys, the ordering of these statements is critical. Since `ArticleCategory`'s table references the corresponding tables of Article and Category, it must be created after the tables it depends on.

At runtime, when ORMLite is first used to operate on the database, the `onCreate()` method will be called. At that time, looking at the `logcat` output will show us the exact statements used in the create process, for example:

```
INFO/TableUtils(2075): executed create table statement changed 1 rows:
CREATE TABLE 'categories'
('parent' integer references categories(_id) on delete cascade,
'name' VARCHAR NOT NULL , '_id' INTEGER PRIMARY KEY AUTOINCREMENT )
```

Implementing the `onUpgrade()` method will vary per application per upgrade. The simplest implementation involves dropping each table with `TableUtils.dropTable()` and then calling `onCreate()`. While perfectly suitable for development time, please be careful to ensure users do not incur data loss in a production environment. A solid implementation would likely transform data to the new schema, execute alter table statements if needed, and only drop a table if it's no longer required.

Finally, because we're targeting API Level 8 and up with this application, we can use foreign keys. However, foreign keys are not enabled by default. Doing so requires executing one line of SQL, which we can do when the database is opened by overriding `onOpen()`, as follows:

```
@Override
public void onOpen(SQLiteDatabase db) {
  super.onOpen(db);
  db.execSQL("PRAGMA foreign_keys=ON;");
}
```

41.5 *Singleton pattern for database access*

We'll use our completed subclass of `OrmLiteSqliteOpenHelper` as a singleton in our host application. By maintaining a single instance of the helper class, our application will have a single connection to its SQLite database. In practice, this will eliminate the dangers of having multiple connections writing at the same time, which can result in failures at runtime.

Our model here includes one process, which has exactly one instance of our subclass, called `DatabaseHelper`. This instance can be used safely from multiple threads due to Java locking that Android does under the hood. Our implementation of the singleton pattern will look like this (with the nonsingleton parts omitted for brevity):

```
public class DatabaseHelper extends OrmLiteSqliteOpenHelper {
  public static final String DATABASE_NAME = "demo.db";
  private static final int DATABASE_VERSION = 1;

  private static DatabaseHelper instance;
```

```
public static synchronized DatabaseHelper getInstance(Context c) {
  if (instance == null)
    instance = new DatabaseHelper(c);

  return instance;
}

private DatabaseHelper(Context context) {
  super(context, DATABASE_NAME, null, DATABASE_VERSION);    ◁┐
  }
}
```

Specifies filename and its version number

In the private constructor, we specify the filename of the database and its version number. The version number passed in the constructor works in conjunction with the `onUpgrade()` method mentioned in the earlier section.

41.6 *CRUD operations made easy*

Database developers will commonly refer to the abbreviation CRUD (create, read, update, and delete) when talking about requirements for an application. We'll explore how to do these operations for the Java classes we implemented as part of this application.

Accessing our objects from the database will be done through an ORMLite class called a DAO (data access object). A DAO is a generic class with the type of the persisted class, and the type of its `ID` field. In the case of our cross-reference objects that don't have an `ID`, such as `ArticleCategory`, we'll use `Void` for this type. On our `DatabaseHelper` singleton, we can obtain a DAO for each class using the `getDao()` method, passing in the appropriate class. For convenience, you may find it helpful to cast the result to use your actual generics, as in the following example. We'll use that convention extensively in the demo application:

```
public class DatabaseHelper extends OrmLiteSqliteOpenHelper {

  /* Remainder omitted */

  public Dao<Article, Integer> getArticleDao() throws SQLException {
    return getDao(Article.class);
  }
}
```

After a DAO is obtained, it exposes a number of methods for creating, updating, deleting, and querying for objects. To create a `Category` record in the database, for example, we simply create a `Category` instance, fill out the information we want persisted, and call the `create()` method on the DAO. ORMLite will then set the `ID` field of our object that was assigned by the database. Suppose we wanted to create two categories, one nested in the other. We can do so like this:

```
Category tutorials = new Category();           ◁─── Create our object
tutorials.setName("Tutorials");

DatabaseHelper helper = DatabaseHelper.getInstance(context);
Dao<Category, Integer> categoryDao = helper.getCategoryDao();    ◁┘

categoryDao.create(tutorials);                 ◁─── Actual create call
```

Get an instance of DatabaseHelper singleton

```
Category programmingTutorials;
String title = "Programming Tutorials";
programmingTutorials = new Category(title, tutorials);
categoryDao.create(programmingTutorials);
```

> **Tutorials object has its ID set, so it's used as parent in new category**

Reading a single object given its ID field is as simple as calling the queryForId() method on the DAO. The DAO objects also expose updates and deletes to single objects just as easily. By passing in an instance with its ID field already set, these operations are just as easy. Suppose we know the ID of the first item created in the previous snippet. We can rename it as follows:

```
Category renamed = new Category(1, "Android Tutorials", null);
categoryDao.update(renamed);
```

We can also delete objects similarly:

```
Category toDelete = new Category();
toDelete.setId(2);
categoryDao.delete(toDelete);
```

When updating, it's important that the source object has all appropriate member variables filled out. When deleting, all that's required is the ID. In the above example, we could, of course, have passed in the original instances tutorials and programming-Tutorials to the update and delete methods respectively.

41.7 Query builders

Operating on a single record in a database is as simple as it gets, and we can express more complicated queries that return multiple records and update and delete many records, as well, using the QueryBuilder, UpdateBuilder, and DeleteBuilder classes, all available from a DAO object by calling queryBuilder(), updateBuilder(), and deleteBuilder(), respectively.

First, let's write a query that will return the names of all to-level categories in the database. We'll use the same DAO object as before, of type Dao<Category, Integer>:

```
PreparedQuery<Category> query = categoryDao.queryBuilder()
                .selectColumns(Category.NAME_COLUMN)
                .where()
                .isNull(Category.PARENT_COLUMN)
                .prepare();
List<Category> topLevelNames = categoryDao.query(query);
```

The methods on the QueryBuilder class can be used to form a query using the typical SQL operators. You can use combinations of and(), or(), eq() for equals, not(), ge() for greater than or equals, and so on to form your where clause. The QueryBuilder and its update and delete counterparts use a fluent interface, meaning each method returns a reference to the same object, so developers will typically "chain" calls together for readability purposes.

In this example, we also do a projection by calling selectColumns() and specifying only the columns we want filled in on our resulting objects (just the name). After expressing our query, we call prepare() on the QueryBuilder, resulting in a typed PreparedQuery instance. Passing the result to the query() method will return our top-level categories.

Continuing with builders, let's look at some more examples. Suppose we want to count the number of child categories given an ID of the parent, which we denote as a variable, parentId. We can use another method exposed by the QueryBuilder to signal that we're performing a count operation, setCountOf(). Then we use the countOf() method on our DAO:

```
PreparedQuery<Category> countQuery = categoryDao.queryBuilder()
                    .setCountOf(true)
                    .where()
                    .eq(Category.PARENT_COLUMN, parentId)
                    .prepare();
long children = categoryDao.countOf(countQuery);
```

Delete operations are very similar. Suppose we want to run a delete statement to remove any articles that are older than 30 days. We can do that using the Delete-Builder class, as in the following example:

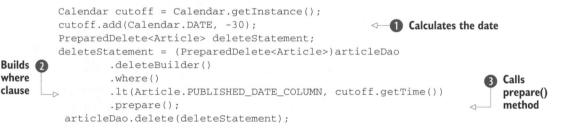

```
Calendar cutoff = Calendar.getInstance();
cutoff.add(Calendar.DATE, -30);                            ①  Calculates the date
PreparedDelete<Article> deleteStatement;
deleteStatement = (PreparedDelete<Article>)articleDao
            .deleteBuilder()
Builds ②   .where()                                        ③  Calls
where       .lt(Article.PUBLISHED_DATE_COLUMN, cutoff.getTime())   prepare()
clause      .prepare();                                             method
  articleDao.delete(deleteStatement);
```

Let's dissect the example. We first calculate the date that is 30 days prior ①. We use the lt() function to build our where clause ②, specifying that we should delete values that are less than the given date. Finally, after calling the prepare() method ③, we must typecast this to a PreparedDelete. The reason for this is that the delete() method on our DAO doesn't accept a PreparedQuery, which is the type that prepare() will return. We know ahead of time that this cast is correct. Note that in comparison operations, such as less-than, we must be careful to pass to the ORM the same type as we defined in our class. Here we pass in a Date, which corresponds to the member variable on the Article class:

```
private Date publishedDate;
```

Now, when an article is deleted, we must ensure that our data integrity is maintained. In this case, that means the IDs we delete with this statement should no longer appear in the Article to Category cross-reference table, and similarly, the IDs shouldn't appear in the Comment class's table. Fortunately for us, our delete statement also has a hidden feature. Because we took care when designing our database schema earlier, we specified a cascading delete on the `ArticleCategory` class to take care of this for us. We can also use the same strategy when implementing the `Comment` class. Thus, the above delete query is all that's needed to delete articles including any comments and their mappings to categories.

These examples are just some of the types of statements we can form using the builder objects. A full application will likely contain many more combinations of selecting data and performing inserts, updates, and deletes. Furthermore, we have yet to touch on the tricky subject of handling foreign object references and the options available when querying for data stored in different tables.

41.8 *Data types and tricky foreign types*

Up until this point, we've let ORMLite handle mapping our Java types to SQLite storage classes. We also haven't shown complex queries that include data from more than one table. Fortunately, ORMLite allows us to tune its behavior using the same annotations we used when setting up our database schema.

The simplest change we can make is changing the storage class of a member variable, such as a date. By default, ORMLite will map the type `java.util.Date` to VARCHAR and store dates in the `yyyy-MM-dd HH:mm:ss.SSSSSS` format. If, for example, we wish to store dates as a number (as in number of milliseconds since the epoch), we can use the following modified annotation from the `Article` class:

```
@DatabaseField(canBeNull = false, dataType = DataType.DATE_LONG,
 columnName = PUBLISHED_DATE_COLUMN)
private Date publishedDate;
```

This will result in a create table statement that uses the `BIGINT` storage class.

Now, let's handle the case of a foreign object. We know that a `Category` can have a parent, but how should the ORM behave when we retrieve a `Category` that has one? Should the parent in its entirety be returned? What about the parent's parent? ORMLite introduces `foreign auto refresh` to specify this behavior and `foreign refresh level` to configure it. In the default scenario, querying for a category will result in the parent being set, with only the `ID` field populated. The default behavior here will be the most efficient in terms of the SQL queries performed by the ORM. When enabling the auto-refresh features, developers should be aware of a potentially large amount of statements being executed, since the version at the time of writing (4.41) doesn't perform joins, but instead, executes additional statements.

Here's a concrete example for a one-to-one relation. Suppose we always want a `Category`'s parent refreshed. We can set `foreignAutoRefresh = true` on the annotation of the parent member variable, such as this:

```
@DatabaseField(foreign = true, foreignAutoRefresh = true,
  canBeNull = true, columnName = PARENT_COLUMN,
  columnDefinition = "integer references " + TABLE_NAME +
  "(" + ID_COLUMN + ") on delete cascade")
private Category parent;
```

When enabling this feature, ORMLite will by default perform two levels of refresh. With the above definition of the annotation, ORMLite will populate a `Category`, its parent, and its grandparent (if available). The default of 2 can be changed using the `maxForeignAutoRefreshLevel` element of the annotation. If anything, changing this value to 1 would be the most likely change (again, increasing this value will result in more SQL queries being executed).

Now, suppose we're interested in a relation that is one-to-many, as in the case of one `Article` with potentially many comments. We can introduce a member variable on the `Article` class and annotate it as a `ForeignCollectionField`. We can use this field to either selectively refresh all the comments, or have it automatically happen when an article is loaded, as specified by the eager element. Here's an example:

```
@DatabaseTable(tableName = Article.TABLE_NAME)
public class Article {

  ...

  @ForeignCollectionField(eager = true)
  private ForeignCollection<Comment> comments;

}
```

With this definition, ORMLite won't add any extra columns to the generated table for the `Article` class. Instead, it will spin up a DAO and query for all the comments associated with each article. As you can imagine, this may be costly when querying for many articles if each article has many comments. Thus, we'll see how to work with a non-eager collection, which can be tricky. Let's remove the `eager = true` element from our annotation (false is the default):

```
@ForeignCollectionField
private ForeignCollection<Comment> comments;
```

Now, ORMLite won't query for the associated comments by default. However, we must be careful when dealing with the comments variable, since its type is `ForeignCollection`. When the collection is non-eager, invoking any method on the collection will cause I/O, such as `size()` and `iterator()`. Also, our debugger may be calling `iterator()` for us, resulting in unexpected I/O and a strangely populated collection when we didn't expect it. The ORMLite documentation recommends populating a collection of this form by using the `toArray()` method on the collection. Here's one example of loading a single article, and then all of its comments:

```
DatabaseHelper helper = DatabaseHelper.getInstance(context);
Dao<Article, Integer> articleDao = helper.getArticleDao();

Article article;
article = articleDao.queryForId(1);          ◁—— Load single article

Comment[] comments;
comments = article.getComments().toArray(new Comment[0]);   ◁—— Load all comments
```

Last, please consult the documentation (http://mng.bz/84k8) on properly calling `close()` on an iterator, such as one obtained from a `ForeignCollection`.

41.9   *Raw SQL queries*

Writing out a SQL query can often be much more efficient than relying on the ORM to build and execute the needed queries. This comes into play when dealing with data stored in multiple tables, as in the case with foreign objects discussed earlier. In performance-critical areas, it's more efficient to write a SQL join rather than relying on the DAO methods to automatically or selectively refresh objects.

Performing a raw SQL query involves first obtaining a DAO, and then using one overload of the queryRaw() method. Each signature of the queryRaw() method expects a variable number of strings as the last parameter. This is to allow developers to parameterize queries and have the ORM handle escaping the values. This is extremely important when performing queries based on user input; otherwise, your database will be open to SQL injection attacks.

The overloads of queryRaw() allow us to fine-tune exactly what we receive as the result for our queries. Our choices are

- A list of string arrays, one array per result, in which each array holds the raw string values of the columns selected
- A list of object arrays, one array per result, which are typed based on our input
- A list of fully baked class instances, given a parameterized RawRowMapper

We'll demo the RawRowMapper case, because it involves the most explanation, yet often results in code that is easiest to reuse. Suppose we want a list of all the articles in the database along with their category names (along with IDs). Using the ORM to perform this operation would result in an amount of queries that is proportional to the number of entries in the database. We can do better by using one query that joins three tables, namely, the tables for Article, Category, and the cross-reference class ArticleCategory. Our query will be this:

```
select a.title, a._id, c.name, c._id from articles a, categories c,
  articlecategories ac
  where ac.article_id = a._id and ac.category_id = c._id;
```

First, let's define a class to hold our results:

```
class ArticleCategoryName {
    public String articleTitle, categoryName;
    public Integer articleId, categoryId;
}
```

Next, we implement the RawRowMapper, which will be invoked on each record returned by our query. Its job is to turn the raw string array representing the columns returned by the database into an instance of our desired type, which is Article-CategoryName in this case (note the use of generics):

```
class ArticleWithCategoryMapper
  implements RawRowMapper<ArticleCategoryName> {

  @Override
  public ArticleCategoryName mapRow(String[] columnNames,
    String[] resultColumns) throws SQLException {
```

```
     ArticleCategoryName result = new ArticleCategoryName();
     result.articleTitle = resultColumns[0];
     result.articleId = Integer.parseInt(resultColumns[1]);
     result.categoryName = resultColumns[2];
     result.categoryId = Integer.parseInt(resultColumns[3]);

     return result;
   }
 }
```

When parsing results in the `mapRow()` method, it's important to check for data consistency. Putting all the components together, we can get a list of all the article names and their categories using this:

```
GenericRawResults<ArticleCategoryName> rawResults;
String query = "select a.title, a._id, c.name, c._id from articles a,
  categories c, articlecategories ac
  where ac.article_id = a._id and ac.category_id = c._id";
ArticleWithCategoryMapper mapper = new ArticleWithCategoryMapper();
rawResults = articleDao.queryRaw(query, mapper);
List<ArticleCategoryName> results = rawResults.getResults();
```

41.10 *Transactions*

Transactions are a key component in database operations, because they allow multiple statements to be treated as a single atomic unit. A transaction guarantees that one of two possibilities will happen:

- All statements will be executed and committed if no errors are encountered.
- If an error is encountered at any point in a transaction, the entire transaction is rolled back.

As a convenience, ORMLite provides a class called `TransactionManager` that wraps the details of beginning a transaction, marking one as successful, and ending a transaction. A `TransactionManager` exposes just one interesting method, which is `callInTransaction()`. This method accepts a `Callable`, which is just like a `Runnable`, except `Callable` has a return value.

To run a transaction, we choose to expose this feature as a method of our `OrmLiteSqliteOpenHelper` subclass, `DatabaseHelper`:

```
public class DatabaseHelper extends OrmLiteSqliteOpenHelper {

  public <T> T callInTransaction(Callable<T> callback) {
    try {
      TransactionManager manager;
      manager = new TransactionManager(getConnectionSource());
      return manager.callInTransaction(callback);

    } catch (SQLException e) {
      Log.e(TAG, "Exception occurred in transaction.", e);
      throw new RuntimeException(e);
    }
  }
}
```

Running a transaction is as simple as putting our database operations inside a `Call-able`. Here's an example method that performs two writes inside a transaction and returns the resulting `Article`:

```
public Article ████████████████████████(Context context,
    final String title, final String text, final Category category) {

    final DatabaseHelper helper = DatabaseHelper.getInstance(context);
    return helper.callInTransaction(new Callable<Article>() {
        @Override
        public Article call() throws SQLException {
            Article article = new Article(new Date(), text, title);

            Dao<Article, Integer> articleDao;
            articleDao = helper.getArticleDao();
            articleDao.create(article);

            Dao<ArticleCategory, Void> articleCategoryDao;
            articleCategoryDao = helper.getArticleCategoryDao();

            articleCategoryDao.create(new ArticleCategory(article, category));

            return article;
        }
    });
}
```

Add it to database using a DAO

Make new instance of Article

Add cross-reference entry

We chose to use a transaction in this case because we want both write operations to succeed, or in the case of failure, to have no writes committed. This approach is recommended when performing multiple writes, for data consistency. Additionally, transactions can in some cases increase the performance of a combination of statements, especially a mix of reads and writes.

41.11 *The bottom line*

ORMLite can greatly simplify database development in an Android application. It can be used to create an entire database instance just by properly annotating your Java classes. It also handles mapping database queries to instances of your classes, removing the need for boilerplate code.

For performance-critical operations that involve multiple tables, consider writing join statements by hand, and use the `queryRaw()` method on a DAO. This, in practice, will be much more efficient than querying additional tables one by one, as in the case of ORM-generated statements. Furthermore, consider using transactions to batch together several writes to ensure data consistency. Last, a singleton pattern is encouraged for your subclass of `SQLiteOpenHelper` to eliminate problems when writing from multiple threads.

41.12 *External links*

http://ormlite.com/javadoc/ormlite-core/doc-files/ormlite_1.html
http://ormlite.com/javadoc/ormlite-core/doc-files/ormlite_2.html#IDX195
http://touchlabblog.tumblr.com/post/24474750219/single-sqlite-connection

Hack 42 *Creating custom functions in SQLite*
Android v1.6+

Android uses SQLite for its databases. Although it offers a good API, you'll sometimes feel a bit limited. What would you do if you want to sort results using a comparator? Did you ever try to implement a query that returns the distance between two GPS coordinates? One of SQLite's biggest limitations is its lack of math functions, making some queries impossible to achieve.

In this hack, I'll show you how to use the Android NDK to provide custom functions to your SQLite queries. We'll create an application that uses a custom SQLite function to calculate distances from different POIs (points of interest) in a database. This function will use the GPS coordinates of the POIs and the haversine formula to return the distance in kilometers.

We can see the application running in figure 42.1. In this figure, we see that different POIs from France were added. Later, the user searches using the Notre Dame de Paris' GPS coordinates and the distance to the different POIs is shown.

Figure 42.1   Distance from Notre Dame to different POIs in France

To make this work, we'll use the Android NDK. We'll use Java to create POIs and insert them in the database using the ordinary `SQLiteOpenHelper` class, but when the user searches the database we'll use an NDK call. We'll first see how to handle the Java part, and afterward we'll see the NDK code.

42.1   Java code

The idea to make this work correctly is to keep doing the simple database queries using the Java API and only use the NDK when we need to use a custom function. The interesting code in the Java part is the `DatabaseHelper` class. This class will be in charge of calling the NDK code when necessary.

Let's check the `DatabaseHelper`'s code:

```
public class DatabaseHelper extends SQLiteOpenHelper {
  public static final String DATABASE_NAME = "pois.db";
  private static final int DATABASE_VERSION = 1;
  private Context mContext;

  static {
    System.loadLibrary("hack042-native");          ◁──❶ Load native library
  }

  public DatabaseHelper(Context context) {
```

```
    super(context, DATABASE_NAME, null, DATABASE_VERSION);
    mContext = context;
}

@Override
public void onCreate(SQLiteDatabase db) {
    db.execSQL("CREATE TABLE " +
        "pois (" +
        "_id INTEGER PRIMARY KEY AUTOINCREMENT," +
        "title TEXT," +
        "longitude FLOAT," +
        "latitude FLOAT);");
}

@Override
public void onUpgrade(SQLiteDatabase db, int oldVersion,
    int newVersion) {
    db.execSQL("DROP TABLE IF EXISTS pois;");

}

public List<Poi>getNear(float latitude, float longitude) {
    File file = mContext.getDatabasePath(DATABASE_NAME);
    return getNear(file.getAbsolutePath(), latitude, longitude);
}

private native List<Poi> getNear(String dbPath, float latitude,
    float longitude);
}
```

② POIs table schema

③ getNear() Java implementation

④ getNear() native implementation signature

The fist important line is loading the native library **①**. System.loadLibrary() is usually called from a static block. This means that when the class is loaded, it will also load the native library called hack042-native. In the onCreate() method **②**, we can learn what the database schema looks like. Our DatabaseHelper class contains a get-Near() **③** method that will be called when the user clicks on the Search button. This method is just a wrapper for its native version **④**. The Java version is the public one because the native implementation needs the database path, and only the Database-Helper class knows where it is.

42.2 Native code

We'll use the NDK to query our database when we need to use custom functions. To do so, we'll need to be able to operate with SQLite from the NDK, and that means we'll need to compile it. Fortunately, it's easier than you would expect. We simply add .c and .h file extensions. Adding sqlite3.c to the LOCAL_SRC_FILES inside the Android.mk file is enough to use it.

Inside main.cpp we have all the NDK code. We'll need to do the following:

- Use JNI to create Java objects.
- Use the SQLite's C/C++ API to query our database.
- Return a List<Poi> as a jobject.

Let's take a look at the implementation of getNear():

```
jobject Java_com_manning_androidhacks_hack042_db_DatabaseHelper_getNear(
  JNIEnv *env, jobject thiz, jstring dbPath,
  jfloat lat, jfloat lon) {

  sqlite3 *db;
  sqlite3_stmt *stmt;
  const char *path = env->GetStringUTFChars(dbPath, 0);

  jclass arrayClass = env->FindClass("java/util/ArrayList");
  jmethodID mid_init =  env->GetMethodID(arrayClass, "<init>", "()V");
  jobject objArr = env->NewObject(arrayClass, mid_init);
  jmethodID mid_add = env->GetMethodID(arrayClass, "add",    "(Ljava/lang/
    Object;)Z");
  jclass poiClass = env->FindClass(
    "com.manning.androidhacks.hack042.model.Poi");
  jmethodID poi_mid_init =  env->GetMethodID(poiClass, "<init>",
    "(Ljava/lang/String;FFF)V");

  sqlite3_open(path, &db);
  env->ReleaseStringUTFChars(dbPath, path);

  sqlite3_create_function(db, "distance", 4, SQLITE_UTF8,
    NULL, &distanceFunc, NULL, NULL);

  if (sqlite3_prepare(db,
    "SELECT title, latitude, longitude,
      distance(latitude, longitude, ?, ?) as kms
      FROM pois ORDER BY kms",
    -1, &stmt, NULL) == SQLITE_OK) {
      int err;
      sqlite3_bind_double(stmt, 1, lat);
      sqlite3_bind_double(stmt, 2, lon);

      while ((err = sqlite3_step(stmt)) == SQLITE_ROW) {
          const char *name = (char const *)
            sqlite3_column_text(stmt, 0);
          jfloat latitude = sqlite3_column_double(stmt, 1);
          jfloat longitude = sqlite3_column_double(stmt, 2);
          jfloat distance = sqlite3_column_double(stmt, 3);

          jobject poiObj = env->NewObject(poiClass,
              poi_mid_init,
              env->NewStringUTF(name),
              latitude,
              longitude,
              distance);

          env->CallBooleanMethod(objArr, mid_add, poiObj);
      }

      if (err != SQLITE_DONE) {
          LOGI("Query execution failed: %s\n", sqlite3_errmsg(db));
      }

      sqlite3_finalize(stmt);

  } else {
```

Annotations:
- getNear() native method ➊
- ArrayList creation ➋
- Open database with a certain path ➌
- Create custom function ➍
- Create query ➎
- Iterate through results ➏
- Create new Poi object ➐

```
        LOGI("Can't execute query: %s\n", sqlite3_errmsg(db));
    }

    return objArr;
}
```

The first thing to notice is the difference between the Java and NDK signatures ❶. Since we need to return a List<Poi>, we create a new ArrayList using JNI ❷. After that, we can open the database using the path provided ❸ and create a custom function passing a function pointer ❹. The distance() function is defined inside the main.cpp file. After the custom function is created, we can write our query using the distance() function ❺. The final step is iterating through the results ❻, create a Poi object using the row data ❼, and add it to the list.

Now that we have all the native code in place, whenever we call the Database-Helper's getNear() method, it will use the custom function created in this section.

42.3   *The bottom line*

Using the NDK might sound like a lot of work, but doing so will give you more flexibility. You might be thinking that instead of returning an array from native code, you could query the database through Java, calculate the distance and sort after doing the query. This is true, but if the database is big enough, using an array wouldn't work. The best way to solve this is returning a Cursor from the native code. The implementation to return a Cursor would be much harder to code, but someone already did it. You can check the android-database-sqlcipher source code; it's already implemented there. When you have a Cursor, you'll be able to use a CursorAdapter as an adapter for your ListView, making everything extremely easy.

You should also know that there's a way to avoid creating custom functions. You can precalculate values and insert them into the row. This might be sufficient, depending on the type of queries your application does.

42.4   *External links*

http://en.wikipedia.org/wiki/Haversine_formula

http://developer.android.com/reference/android/database/sqlite/
     package-summary.html

www.sqlite.org/capi3.html

www.movable-type.co.uk/scripts/latlong.html

www.thismuchiknow.co.uk/?p=71

https://github.com/sqlcipher/android-database-sqlcipher

Hack 43　*Batching database operations*
Android v2.1+

A good pattern inside Android applications is to save your data inside a database and show it in a `ListView` using a `CursorAdapter`. If you use a `ContentProvider` to handle the database operations, you can return a `Cursor` that will be updated whenever the data changes. This means that if you do everything correctly, you can work on the logic to modify the information inside a table from a background thread and the UI will update automagically. The problem with this approach is that when you do a large number of operations to the database, your `Cursor` will get updated frequently, making your UI flicker.

In this hack, we'll see how to use batch operations to avoid this flickering, creating three possible implementations to understand the problem and find a solution:

- Without batching
- With batching
- With batching and using the `SQLiteContentProvider` class

The demo application is simple. It shows a list of numbers from 1 to 100. When the user clicks on the Refresh button, the old numbers are deleted and new ones are created. To accomplish this, we'll code three different implementations of the following:

- An `Activity` to display the numbers
- An `Adapter` to create and populate the views for the `ListView`
- A `ContentProvider` to handle queries to the database
- A `Service` that will update the table through the `ContentProvider`

You can see the finished application in figure 43.1. Each row shows the database ID on the left and the generated number on the right.

As you an imagine, most of the code for the three solutions is similar. Every implementation will have its own `Activity`, `Adapter`, `Service`, and `Content-Provider`. Since you can go through the sample code, here we'll only discuss the differences, which reside in the `Service` and in the `ContentProvider`.

Figure 43.1　List with numbers

43.1　*No batch*

This is the simplest example. Inside the `Service`, we just hit the `ContentProvider` whenever we want to do an operation to the table. Here's the `Service` code:

```
public class NoBatchService extends IntentService {

  ...

  @Override
  protected void onHandleIntent(Intent intent) {

    ContentResolver contentResolver = getContentResolver();
    contentResolver.delete(
      NoBatchNumbersContentProvider.CONTENT_URI,
      null, null);

    for (int i = 1; i <= 100; i++) {
      ContentValues cv = new ContentValues();
      cv.put(
        NoBatchNumbersContentProvider.COLUMN_TEXT, "" + i);
      contentResolver.insert(
        NoBatchNumbersContentProvider.CONTENT_URI, cv);
    }
  }
}
```

> Before inserting new numbers, delete all old ones.

> Inside the for loop create ContentValue and insert number using ContentResolver.

Try running the application and test this implementation. The best way of noticing the flickering is clicking on the Refresh button and trying to scroll over the list of numbers. You'll find out that it's very difficult to scroll.

This happens because every time we do an insert or a delete using the NoBatchNumbersContentProvider, it does this:

```
getContext().getContentResolver().notifyChange(uri, null);
```

This means that every Cursor retrieved from NoBatchNumbersContentProvider's query() method will be updated and the Adapter will make the ListView refresh itself.

43.2 *Using batch operations*

The second approach is using batch operations. Inside the ContentProvider class, we have the following method:

```
public ContentProviderResult[] applyBatch(
    ArrayList<ContentProviderOperation> operations);
```

The idea is to create a list of ContentProviderOperations and apply them all together. In this case, the Service looks like this:

```
public class BatchService extends IntentService {
  private static final String TAG =
    BatchService.class.getCanonicalName();

  ...

  @Override
  protected void onHandleIntent(Intent intent) {
    Builder builder = null;
    ContentResolver contentResolver = getContentResolver();
    ArrayList<ContentProviderOperation> operations =
        new ArrayList<ContentProviderOperation>();
```

> Create list of ContentProviderOperations.

Create delete operation using ContentProvider-Operation's Builder and add it to list of operations to apply.

```
builder = ContentProviderOperation
    .newDelete(BatchNumbersContentProvider.CONTENT_URI);
operations.add(builder.build());

for (int i = 1; i <= 100; i++) {
  ContentValues cv = new ContentValues();
  cv.put(NoBatchNumbersContentProvider.COLUMN_TEXT, "" + i);

  builder = ContentProviderOperation
      .newInsert(BatchNumbersContentProvider.CONTENT_URI);
  builder.withValues(cv);

  operations.add(builder.build());
}
try {
  contentResolver.applyBatch(
      BatchNumbersContentProvider.AUTHORITY, operations);
} catch (RemoteException e) {
  Log.e(TAG, "Couldn't apply batch: " + e.getMessage());
} catch (OperationApplicationException e) {
  Log.e(TAG, "Couldn't apply batch: " + e.getMessage());
}
  }
}
```

Create an insert operation per number.

With list of operations created, call applyBatch() method.

If you test this approach, you won't notice any difference: the flickering is still there. Why?

If you go to Android's `ContentProvider` implementation, you'll notice that the `applyBatch()` method doesn't do anything in particular. It just iterates through the operations and calls the `apply()` method, which will end up calling our `insert()` / `delete()` methods inside the `BatchNumbersContentProvider` class.

All this might sound awkward, but it's exactly what the `applyBatch()` method documentation says (see section 43.5):

> Override this to handle requests to perform a batch of operations, or the default implementation will iterate over the operations and call apply(ContentProvider, ContentProviderResult[], int) on each of them. If all calls to apply(ContentProvider, Content-Provider-Result[], int) succeed then a ContentProvider-Result array with as many elements as there were operations will be returned. If any of the calls fail, it is up to the implementation how many of the others take effect.

43.3 *Applying batch using SQLiteContentProvider*

We already know that applying the changes in batch is the solution for our problem and we also know that we need to somehow modify the `applyBatch()` method inside our `ContentProvider` implementation to make this work. Fortunately, someone already did it.

There's a class inside the Android Open Source Project (AOSP) called SQLite-ContentProvider that doesn't belong to the SDK. It's inside com.android.providers .calendar. For this case, instead of extending ContentProvider, we'll extend from SQLiteContentProvider.

The service code is exactly the same as the second approach, so let's look inside the SQLiteContentProvider's applyBatch() method:

```
@Override
public ContentProviderResult[] applyBatch(
    ArrayList<ContentProviderOperation> operations)
    throws OperationApplicationException {                All operations are
  mDb = mOpenHelper.getWritableDatabase();                applied inside database
  mDb.beginTransactionWithListener(this);                 transaction.

  try {
    mApplyingBatch.set(true);
    final int numOperations = operations.size();
    final ContentProviderResult[] results =
      new ContentProviderResult[numOperations];

    for (int i = 0; i < numOperations; i++) {
      final ContentProviderOperation operation = operations.get(i);
      results[i] = operation.apply(this, results, i);       Implementation
    }                                                        also calls apply().

    mDb.setTransactionSuccessful();            Finish database
    return results;                            transaction.

  } finally {
    mApplyingBatch.set(false);          onEndTransaction takes care
    mDb.endTransaction();               of notifying changes after all
    onEndTransaction();                 operations applied.
  }
}
```

So far, we know that every operation is applied inside a database transaction, but this implementation still calls the apply() method for every operation. Why wouldn't we get a notification for every insert() / delete()?

To understand why this works correctly, we need to read the SQLiteContent-Provider's insert() method:

```
@Override
public Uri insert(Uri uri, ContentValues values) {
  Uri result = null;                                   Check if we're
  boolean applyingBatch = applyingBatch();             applying a batch.

  if (!applyingBatch) {
    mDb = mOpenHelper.getWritableDatabase();
    mDb.beginTransactionWithListener(this);
    try {
      result = insertInTransaction(uri, values);
      if (result != null) {
        mNotifyChange = true;
      }
      mDb.setTransactionSuccessful();
```

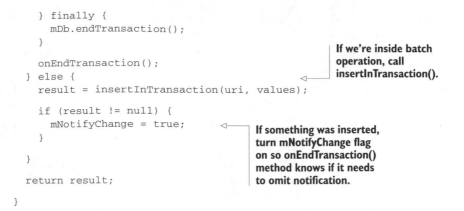

```
      } finally {
        mDb.endTransaction();
      }

      onEndTransaction();
    } else {
      result = insertInTransaction(uri, values);

      if (result != null) {
        mNotifyChange = true;
      }

    }

    return result;

  }
```

If we're inside batch operation, call insertInTransaction().

If something was inserted, turn mNotifyChange flag on so onEndTransaction() method knows if it needs to omit notification.

The logic for `insertInTransaction()` is inside our implementation. It's the same as the others, but it lacks the notification logic.

If you run this implementation, you'll see how the flicker disappeared because the UI will only be refreshed when all the operations get applied.

43.4 *The bottom line*

It's a shame that the `SQLiteContentProvider` class doesn't belong to the SDK. If your `ContentProvider` is using a `SQLite` database to store data, give it a try. Your UI will look more responsive and applying operations inside a single transaction will make everything run faster.

43.5 *External links*

http://developer.android.com/reference/android/content/ContentProvider.html

http://stackoverflow.com/questions/9801304/
　　　　android-contentprovider-calls-bursts-of-setnotificationuri-to-cursoradapter-wh

Avoiding fragmentation

Fragmentation is a serious issue for Android developers. In this chapter, we'll look at some tips on how to achieve certain tasks and still be backward compatible with older versions.

Hack 44 Handling lights-out mode
Android v1.6+

Since the early beginnings of Android, the whole system has had a status bar at the top of the screen. In Android Honeycomb, the status bar was moved to the bottom of the screen.

Applications such as games or image viewers need the full attention of the user, and most of them take the whole screen to display themselves. For instance, in the default Gallery application, when you click on an image, it's shown full-screen without any other content.

Imagine you need to provide this feature in your application, and it needs to be compatible with every Android version. In this hack, we'll build a simple toy application that will have a red background and, when we press it, the application will enter lights-out mode. We'll take care of Android 2.x and 3.x separately, but then we'll merge them into a single implementation.

44.1   *Android 2.x*

Let's build the application with Android 2.x code first. In Android 2.x, we have the concept of full-screen mode. The idea behind full-screen mode is to allow the application's window to use the entire display space.

We're also interested in another concept: the application's title. The application's title is the gray bar we get on the upper part of the screen.

Let's look at the code that creates the effect:

```java
public void onCreate(Bundle savedInstanceState) {
  super.onCreate(savedInstanceState);

  requestWindowFeature(Window.FEATURE_NO_TITLE);          ◁─❶ Removes the title bar

  setContentView(R.layout.main);
  mContentView = findViewById(R.id.content);              ◁─┐ Calls and asks
                                                          ❷  for a reference
  mContentView.setOnClickListener(new OnClickListener() {
    @Override
    public void onClick(View v) {
                                                    ❸  How field
      Window w = getWindow();                          variable toggles
      if(mUseFullscreen) {                      ◁─┘    the status
        w.addFlags(
          WindowManager.LayoutParams.FLAG_FULLSCREEN);
        w.clearFlags(
          WindowManager.LayoutParams.FLAG_FORCE_NOT_FULLSCREEN);

      } else {
        w.addFlags(
          WindowManager.LayoutParams.FLAG_FORCE_NOT_FULLSCREEN);
        w.clearFlags(
          WindowManager.LayoutParams.FLAG_FULLSCREEN);
      }

      mUseFullscreen = !mUseFullscreen;
    }
  });
}
```

The code is self-explanatory. We first remove the title bar ❶. This needs to be done before the setContentView() call is made. Afterward, we make an ordinary set-ContentView() call and ask for a reference to the root element of our view ❷. This element will work as an on/off switch for the full-screen mode.

The last part of the code states how the full-screen mode should work. You can see in ❸ how a field variable is used to toggle the status.

44.2   *Android 3.x*

In Android 3.x, the concepts explained for Android 2.x vary a little. The title bar ended up being the action bar on the upper part of the screen, and the status bar went to the bottom of the screen.

An important change in Android 3.x is that there are no physical buttons; they're all placed in the status bar. Because of that, the status bar can't be dismissed, but it can be dimmed.

Here's the code:

```
@Override
public void onCreate(Bundle savedInstanceState) {
  super.onCreate(savedInstanceState);
  setContentView(R.layout.main);
  mContentView = findViewById(R.id.content);                    ❶ Reference to
                                                                   root element

  mContentView.setOnSystemUiVisibilityChangeListener(          ❷ Hides
    new OnSystemUiVisibilityChangeListener() {                     or shows
      public void onSystemUiVisibilityChange(int visibility) {     action bar

        ActionBar actionBar = getActionBar();

        if (actionBar != null) {
          mContentView.setSystemUiVisibility(visibility);
                                                                  ❸ Visibility
          if (visibility == View.STATUS_BAR_VISIBLE) {             parameter
            actionBar.show();
          } else {
            actionBar.hide();
          }
        }
      }
  });
                                                                  ❹ Sets a click
  mContentView.setOnClickListener(new OnClickListener() {           listener
    public void onClick(View v) {

      if (mContentView.getSystemUiVisibility() ==
        View.STATUS_BAR_VISIBLE) {

        mContentView.setSystemUiVisibility(View.STATUS_BAR_HIDDEN);

      } else {
        mContentView.setSystemUiVisibility(View.STATUS_BAR_VISIBLE);
      }
    }
  });
}
```

In a similar way to what we did before, we get a reference to the root element of our view ❶. In Honeycomb, views have a new method called setOnSystemUiVisibility-ChangeListener(). This was created to have a place to receive callbacks when the visibility of the system bar changes. We'll use this method to hide or show the action bar, depending on the visibility parameter ❷, as you can see in ❸. In ❹, we set a click listener to the root view where we toggle the system UI visibility, which basically means turning on and off the lights-out mode.

44.3 *Merging both worlds in a single Activity*

We showed how to handle both scenarios in the different Android versions, but it'd be nice if it were cross-compatible. We can create an `Activity` that checks which Android version the device has and runs the corresponding activity. The code to handle this is the following:

```
Class>?> activity = null;
if ( Build.VERSION.SDK_INT >= Build.VERSION_CODES.HONEYCOMB ) {      ◁  ❶ Checks the
    activity = MainActivity2X.class;                                       Android
} else {                                                                   version
    activity = MainActivity3X.class;
}                                                                    ❷ Start
                                                                       different
startActivity(new Intent(this, activity));      ◁                      Activitys
 finish();
```

We used the `Build` class to check the Android version. The `Build` class has a `VERSION_CODES` ❶ inner class that can be used to check which version the device is running. Based on that, we start different `Activitys` ❷.

44.4 *The bottom line*

You'll find out that everything we did here can be done using styles. Doing it with styles is OK if you're not willing to support this feature dynamically.

You should be aware that hiding the status bar prevents the user from seeing notifications and might cause the user to close your app just to see what's going on. On the other hand, using lights-out mode in Android is a cool way of immersing the user in your application experience.

44.5 *External links*

http://developer.android.com/reference/android/view/WindowManager.html
http://developer.android.com/reference/android/app/ActionBar.html

Hack 45 *Using new APIs in older devices*
Android v1.6+

With every Android release, a new set of APIs is made available. Most of the time, this means that developers will have new ways of showing their content or improving the device's functionality. Commonly, when users acquire a new Android version on their device, they'll want to take advantage of all the benefits that come with the new API, but you may still want users with older versions to be able to continue using your application. Is there a way to start using new APIs and still be backward compatible?

In this hack, we'll see how to use new Android APIs and still be able to run on older devices. We'll create a demo application that shows the number of times it was opened. That information will be persisted with the help of the SharedPreferences class. In the sample, we'll use two APIs that are available in newer Android versions. The first one is a method that became available in Android v9. An apply() method was added to the SharedPreferences.Editor class. The second one is an API that became available in Android API Level 8. It allows us to declare inside the manifest whether we'll allow our application to be installed on the SD card. Users with API Level 8 and up will be able to install the application on the SD card, while others will need to install on the device's internal storage.

45.1 *Using apply() instead of commit()*

To edit a SharedPreferences class, we need to get an Editor and use its different methods to modify the SharedPreferences values. When we finish with all the pertinent modifications, we need to call commit().

Since Android version 9, the SharedPreferences.Editor has an apply() method to be used instead of commit(). What's the difference between those two? Here's the documentation explanation (see section 45.4):

> Unlike commit(), which writes its preferences out to persistent storage synchronously, apply() commits its changes to the in-memory SharedPreferences immediately but starts an asynchronous commit to disk and you won't be notified of any failures.

In short, the apply() method should be used instead of commit() if we don't need the return value of the operation.

Since we want our demo application to be super-responsive, we want to use the apply() method to avoid slow commits to the disk in the UI thread. To accomplish that, we'll borrow Brad Fitzpatrick's code to use the apply() method when it's available and fall back to commit() if it's not. Brad Fitzpatrick is a developer working inside the Android team.

Let's first take a look at our Activity's code:

```
public class MainActivity extends Activity {
  private static final String PREFS_NAME = "main_activity_prefs";
  private static final String TIMES_OPENED_KEY = "times opened_key";
  private static final String TIMES_OPENED_FMT = "Times opened: %d";

  private TextView mTextView;
  private int mTimesOpened;

  @Override
  public void onCreate(Bundle savedInstanceState) {
    super.onCreate(savedInstanceState);

    setContentView(R.layout.main);
    mTextView = (TextView) findViewById(R.id.times_opened);
  }
```

① Sets content view and gets a reference to TextView

```
@Override
protected void onResume() {
  super.onResume();

  SharedPreferences prefs = getSharedPreferences(PREFS_NAME, 0);
  mTimesOpened = prefs.getInt(TIMES_OPENED_KEY, 1);
  mTextView.setText(String.format(TIMES_OPENED_FMT, mTimesOpened));
}

@Override
protected void onPause() {
  super.onPause();

  Editor editor = getSharedPreferences(PREFS_NAME, 0).edit();
  editor.putInt(TIMES_OPENED_KEY, mTimesOpened + 1);
  SharedPreferencesCompat.apply(editor);
  }
}
```

Populates the TextView ❷

Increments the times opened variable ❸

Calls apply() ❹ through the Shared-Preferences-Compat class

We first set the content view and get a reference to the TextView that will hold the information about how many times the app has been opened ❶. In the onResume() method, we get the persisted information from the SharedPreferences and we populate the TextView ❷. Finally, in the onPause() method, we get an Editor from the SharedPreferences and we increment the times opened variable ❸. Note that instead of calling apply() directly, we call it through the SharedPreferencesCompat class ❹.

Let's take a look inside the SharedPreferencesCompat class to learn how it makes everything work:

```
public class SharedPreferencesCompat {
  private static final Method sApplyMethod = findApplyMethod();

  private static Method findApplyMethod() {
    try {
      Class cls = SharedPreferences.Editor.class;
      return cls.getMethod("apply");
    } catch (NoSuchMethodException unused) {
      // fall through
    }
    return null;
  }

  public static void apply(SharedPreferences.Editor editor) {
    if (sApplyMethod != null) {
      try {
        sApplyMethod.invoke(editor);
        return;
      } catch (InvocationTargetException unused) {
        // fall through
      } catch (IllegalAccessException unused) {
        // fall through
      }
    }
    editor.commit();
  }
}
```

Checks availability of ❶ apply() method

Tries to invoke the real apply() method ❷ on Editor

◁─❸ Falls back to commit()

SharedPreferencesCompat uses Java's reflection APIs to check the availability of the apply() method inside the SharedPreferences.Editor class **❶**. If it exists, the method is saved as a static variable. When the apply() method is called, it tries to invoke the real apply() method on the Editor passed as a parameter **❷**. If this call falls, it falls back to commit() **❸**.

45.2 *Storing the app on the SD card*

After the previous section, we got a working application that shows how many times it was opened. Now we'll add everything needed to make it install on the SD card instead of the internal storage.

Since Android version 8, you can add an attribute to your AndroidManifest by the name of android:installLocation. To understand what this does, let's look at the documentation (see section 45.5):

> It's an optional feature you can declare for your application with the android:installLocation manifest attribute. If you do not declare this attribute, your application will be installed on the internal storage only and it cannot be moved to the external storage.

To make it work, we'll need to modify AndroidManifest.xml with the following lines:

```
<?xml version="1.0" encoding="utf-8"?>
<manifest xmlns:android="http://schemas.android.com/apk/res/android"
     package="com.manning.androidhacks.hack045"
     android:versionCode="1"
     android:versionName="1.0"
     android:installLocation="preferExternal">

   <uses-sdk android:minSdkVersion="8"/>
```

❶ Sets android:installLocation to preferExternal

❷ Sets minSdkVersion to 8

We set android:installLocation to preferExternal **❶** so our application gets installed on the SD card if possible. To be able to use this feature, we would need to set the minSdkVersion to 8 **❷**. If we leave the code like that, users won't be able to install it on devices with an API level less than 8. To fix this, we can modify the last line with the following:

```
<uses-sdk android:minSdkVersion="4" android:targetSdkVersion="8" />
```

What we're saying with that line is something like this: "Compile with API Level 8 JARs and use the new APIs, but let the application be installed on devices with API Level 4 onward." Although this works, there are some caveats. Compiling against higher API levels will make available backward-incompatible classes and methods. To give you an example of this, if you call a method that's not available in the running version, you'll get a java.lang.VerifyError exception.

45.3 *The bottom line*

Using a compatibility class like `SharedPreferencesCompat` is common practice among Android developers. I recommend using the oldest supported device while developing to avoid this pitfall. When you find a newer API that won't work in that device, create this type of compatibility class and choose what to do when it's not available.

Also remember that the `targetSdkVersion` is an excellent way of using new Android features without leaving out users with older versions.

45.4 *External links*

http://android-developers.blogspot.com/2010/07/
    how-to-have-your-cupcake-and-eat-it-too.html

http://code.google.com/p/zippy-android/source/browse/trunk/examples/
    SharedPreferencesCompat.java

http://developer.android.com/reference/android/content/
    SharedPreferences.Editor.html#apply()

http://developer.android.com/guide/appendix/install-location.html

http://developer.android.com/reference/android/accounts/AccountManager.html

http://developer.android.com/training/search/backward-compat.html

Hack 46 *Backward-compatible notifications*
Android v1.6+

With the release of the Android version Jelly Bean, a new notification API became available. With this new API, the notifications now have actions. Actions allow the user to react to a notification without needing to enter an application. You can see an example of this in figure 46.1. The missed call notification offers the user two possible actions: call back or send a message to the caller.

If your application uses notifications, it would be a great addition to support actions to improve the user experience. How can we use this new set of APIs but still be backward compatible? In this hack, we'll see how to achieve this using Android's support library.

Figure 46.1   Notifications in Jelly Bean

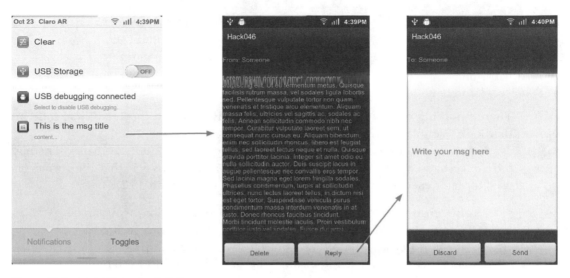

Figure 46.2   Android version 2.3.7

To see how it works, we'll create a demo application that will mock a message application. Because the application will be backward compatible, it will have two possible flows—one using the notifications actions and one without them. To visualize this, you can see the possible flows using a device with Android v2.3.7 (see figure 46.2) without the new notification API, and one with Android v4.1.2 (see figure 46.3).

You'll notice that without the new API, the user is obliged to enter the application. With the new API, users can delete a message without entering the application and they can reply directly without needing to go through the `Activity` holding the message.

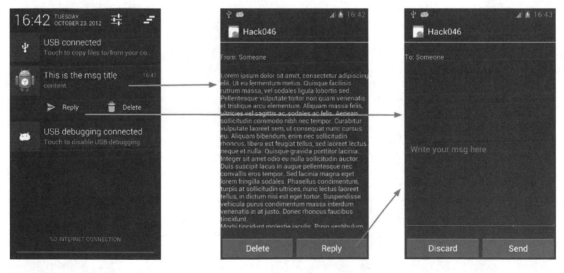

Figure 46.3   Android version 4.1.2

Let's now discuss how to create the application. We'll need three `Activity`s:

- `MainActivity`—This will hold a button to launch the notification.
- `MsgActivity`—The message itself with Reply and Delete buttons.
- `ReplyActivity`—The `Activity` holding the reply `EditText` and the Discard and Send buttons.

There's nothing out of the ordinary in those `Activity`s. You can read their code in this book's sample code.

To handle all of the notification's clicks, we need to use `PendingIntent`s. The big difference between the `PendingIntent` and the `Intent` classes is that the former is used for later execution. From the documentation (see section 46.2):

> By giving a `PendingIntent` to another application, you are granting it the right to perform the operation you have specified as if the other application was yourself (with the same permissions and identity). As such, you should be careful about how you build the `PendingIntent`: often, for example, the base `Intent` you supply will have the component name explicitly set to one of your own components, to ensure it is ultimately sent there and nowhere else.

The limitation to using `PendingIntent`s is that we can't do something like "Run this piece of code." We can only launch an `Activity`, a `Service` or a `BroadcastReceiver`.

We'll need to cover two types of operations in the application—the ones that don't require a UI (delete, discard, send message) and those that do (read, reply to a message). Operations that don't require a UI would ideally require back-end logic, so we'll create a `Service` called `MsgService`.

We'll also create a static class called `NotificationHelper` that will be in charge of all the notification logic and the creation of the `PendingIntent`s. It's code is the following:

```
public class NotificationHelper {

  public static void showMsgNotification(Context ctx) {     ◁─┐ Called by
    final NotificationManager mgr;                             │ MainActivity to
    mgr = (NotificationManager) ctx                            │ show notification
        .getSystemService(Context.NOTIFICATION_SERVICE);

    NotificationCompat.Builder builder =
        new NotificationCompat.Builder(
        ctx).setSmallIcon(android.R.drawable.sym_def_app_icon)
        .setTicker("New msg!").setContentTitle("This is the msg title")
        .setContentText("content...")
        .setContentIntent(getPendingIntent(ctx));

    builder.addAction(android.R.drawable.ic_menu_send,
        ctx.getString(R.string.activity_msg_button_reply),        ◁─┐ Reply
        getReplyPendingIntent(ctx));                                 │ action is
                                                                     │ added
    builder.addAction(android.R.drawable.ic_menu_delete,
        ctx.getString(R.string.activity_msg_button_delete),
        getDeletePendingIntent(ctx));
```

```
        mgr.notify(R.id.activity_main_receive_msg, builder.build());
    }

    private static PendingIntent getDeletePendingIntent(Context ctx) {
        Intent intent = new Intent(ctx, MsgService.class);          ◁──── Delete
        intent.setAction(MsgService.MSG_DELETE);                          PendingIntent will
        intent.setFlags(Intent.FLAG_ACTIVITY_CLEAR_TOP);                 use MsgService
        return PendingIntent.getService(ctx, 0, intent, 0);
    }

    private static PendingIntent getReplyPendingIntent(Context ctx) {
        Intent intent = new Intent(ctx, ReplyActivity.class);      ◁──── Reply
        intent.setFlags(Intent.FLAG_ACTIVITY_CLEAR_TOP);                PendingIntent will
        return PendingIntent.getActivity(ctx, 0, intent, 0);            use ReplyActivity
    }

    private static PendingIntent getPendingIntent(Context ctx) {
        Intent intent = new Intent(ctx, MsgActivity.class);        ◁──── When notification
        intent.setFlags(Intent.FLAG_ACTIVITY_CLEAR_TOP);                is clicked, it will
        return PendingIntent.getActivity(ctx, 0, intent, 0);            use MsgActivity to
    }                                                                   show message

    public static void dismissMsgNotification(Context ctx) {
        final NotificationManager mgr;                             ◁──── Helper method
        mgr = (NotificationManager) ctx                                 to dismiss
            .getSystemService(Context.NOTIFICATION_SERVICE);            notification
        mgr.cancel(R.id.activity_main_receive_msg);
    }
}
```

With the `NotificationHelper` class, we have everything we need to handle the notifications. We'll now analyze part of the `MsgService` code. Because `MsgService` extends
`IntentService`, this is the `onHandleIntent()` method:

```
@Override
protected void onHandleIntent(Intent intent) {
    if ( MSG_RECEIVE.equals(intent.getAction()) ) {
        handleMsgReceive();
    } else if ( MSG_DELETE.equals(intent.getAction()) ) {
        handleMsgDelete();
    } else if ( MSG_REPLY.equals(intent.getAction()) ) {
        handleMsgReply(intent.getStringExtra(MSG_REPLY_KEY));
    }
}
```

We'll have one method per possible action. For the sake of brevity, let's take a look at
`handleMsgDelete()`:

```
private void handleMsgDelete() {                          ❶ Removes a message
    Log.d(TAG, "Removing msg...");                            instead of creates a log
    NotificationHelper.dismissMsgNotification(this);     ◁──── Dismisses
}                                                          ❷ notification
```

In a complete implementation, we'd place some back-end logic to remove a message
instead of creating a log ❶. After the message is deleted, we can dismiss the notification with the help of the `NotificationHelper` class ❷.

We learned how to create a backward-compatible notification and how to handle the different clicks using `PendingIntents`. How can we avoid replication of logic when the `MsgActivity`'s Delete button is pressed? The secret is to let the `MsgService` take care of everything. For example, let's see what the Delete button click handler inside the `MsgActivity` does:

```
public void onDeleteClick(View v) {
  Intent intent = new Intent(this, MsgService.class);
  intent.setAction(MsgService.MSG_DELETE);
  startService(intent);
  finish();
}
```

As you can see, all of the logic is handled inside the `Service`.

46.1 The bottom line

The new notifications API is great. The possibility of performing certain actions from a notification creates new use cases, and with the help of the support library we can make sure we don't leave behind users who run older versions.

46.2 External links

http://developer.android.com/tools/extras/support-library.html
http://developer.android.com/reference/android/app/PendingIntent.html
http://developer.android.com/reference/android/app/IntentService.html

Hack 47 *Creating tabs with fragments*
Android v1.6+

If you've been developing with Android for a while, you've most likely used the `TabActivity` class. This class allows developers to create tabs inside their applications so that users can switch between `Activitys` by pressing the Tab button. The big issue with the `TabActivity` class is that its developer ran into a lot of issues while trying to customize its look, and the class was deprecated with the release of fragments.

Although the Android SDK comes with classes such as `TabHost` and `TabWidget` to handle tabs, creating your own implementation gives you more control over your application. In this hack, I'll show you how to avoid using the `TabActivity` class and instead use fragments to create a tab application. We'll create a toy application that shows a different color in each tab. You can see the finished work in figure 47.1.

Figure 47.1   Custom tabs

47.1 *Creating our tab UI*

The first thing we'll take care of is creating the UI for the tabs. For this task, we'll create our own XML layout for the tabs. Using XML to design our tabs gives us the opportunity to place and size widgets as we like. In this case, we create a LinearLayout with buttons inside it. Here's the XML:

```xml
<?xml version="1.0" encoding="utf-8"?>
<LinearLayout xmlns:android="http://schemas.android.com/apk/res/android"
    android:layout_width="fill_parent"
    android:layout_height="fill_parent"
    android:orientation="horizontal"
    android:background="@null">

    <Button android:id="@+id/tab_red"
        android:layout_height="wrap_content"
        android:layout_width="0dp"
        android:layout_weight="1"
        android:text="Red" />

    <Button android:id="@+id/tab_green"
        android:layout_height="wrap_content"
        android:layout_width="0dp"
        android:layout_weight="1"
        android:text="Green" />

    <Button android:id="@+id/tab_blue"
        android:layout_height="wrap_content"
        android:layout_width="0dp"
        android:layout_weight="1"
        android:text="Blue" />
</LinearLayout>
```

47.2 *Placing the tabs in an Activity*

To avoid copying and pasting the tab layout around every Activity, we'll use the include tag. Here's MainActivity's XML layout:

```xml
<?xml version="1.0" encoding="utf-8"?>
<FrameLayout xmlns:android="http://schemas.android.com/apk/res/android"
    android:orientation="vertical"
    android:layout_width="fill_parent"
    android:layout_height="fill_parent">

    <FrameLayout android:id="@+id/main_fragment_container"     ❶ Fragment
        android:layout_width="fill_parent"                         container
        android:layout_height="fill_parent"/>

    <include layout="@layout/tabs"            ❷ Adds the tabs
        android:layout_width="fill_parent"         layout to
        android:layout_height="wrap_content"/>     Activity's view
</FrameLayout>
```

The FrameLayout in ❶ will be the fragment container. Every time the user presses on a tab, the Activity will take care of placing the corresponding fragment there. In ❷ we use the `include` tag to add the tab's layout to the `Activity`'s view. Note that we place the `include` in the bottom for it to be drawn on top of the fragment container.

We already have all the UI in place. Let's see how we handle the logic from the `Activity`:

```
public class MainActivity extends FragmentActivity {

  @Override
  public void onCreate(Bundle savedInstanceState) {
    super.onCreate(savedInstanceState);
    setContentView(R.layout.main);

    findViewById(R.id.tab_red).setOnClickListener(
      new OnClickListener() {

      @Override
      public void onClick(View v) {
        switchFragment(ColorFragment.newInstance(Color.RED, "Red"));
      }

    });

    ...
  }
  private void switchFragment(Fragment fragment) {
    FragmentTransaction ft;
    ft = getSupportFragmentManager().beginTransaction();
    ft.replace(R.id.main_fragment_container, fragment);
    ft.commit();
  }
}
```

Enable use of ❶ fragments

❷ Button sets click listener that calls switchFragment() with new instance of a fragment

❸ Reads the implementation

As you can see, our `MainActivity` class needs to extend `FragmentActivity` ❶ to be able to use fragments. One of the buttons is fetched and sets a click listener, which will call `switchFragment()` with a new instance of a fragment ❷. Finally, we can read the implementation of the `switchFragment()` method ❸, which performs the logic to place the fragment inside the container.

47.3 *The bottom line*

Creating your own implementation to handle tabs might sound like overkill, but for instance, if your tabs will need fancy animations, I recommend you use an approach similar to what we built in this hack. In the end, it'll be easier to customize it if you have full control over your widgets.

47.4 *External links*

http://developer.android.com/reference/android/app/ActivityGroup.html
http://developer.android.com/reference/android/app/TabActivity.html

Building tools 12

Building software applications often requires custom processes such as adding dependencies, running tests, and deploying in a server. If building from Eclipse feels a bit limiting, you'll find this chapter interesting. We'll cover tips that provide some alternatives for building your applications.

Hack 48 Handling dependencies with Apache Maven
Android v1.6+

The Android SDK comes with a lot of classes and code that help you create your applications, but sometimes even this isn't enough. For example, if you want to add Google Analytics or you want to add a JSON parser, you'll have to add some kind of dependencies. The Android SDK doesn't provide a way to handle dependencies, other than placing JAR files in the /libs folder. Fortunately, it has other building tools. Even if you don't use third-party dependencies, you might want to separate your application in different modules and add dependencies between them in order to organize your code or create reusable components. What you can do to get around this issue is to use Apache Maven. In this hack you'll see how to use Apache Maven to build your application and run tests.

If you've used Maven for Java application dependencies, you'll agree that it's a powerful tool, but it takes some time to get used to it. In this case, we'll take a look at Manfred Moser's roboguice-calculator demo. In this project, Manfred used different dependencies, making it an excellent example to demonstrate how Maven works.

To understand how Maven works, we'll go through the different pom.xml sections. The pom.xml is the only Maven-related file your project will have. In it you'll tell Maven your application name, the build dependencies, the test dependencies, and how to create your APK. Maven first checks if you have the dependencies in the local repository, which is located at ~/.m2/repository by default. If they're not there, it will take care of downloading them from a central repository.

The first part has the following code:

```xml
<?xml version="1.0" encoding="UTF-8"?>
<project xmlns="http://Maven.apache.org/POM/4.0.0"
 xmlns:xsi="http://www.w3.org/2001/XMLSchema-instance"
 xsi:schemaLocation="http://Maven.apache.org/POM/4.0.0
 http://Maven.apache.org/Maven-v4_0_0.xsd">
 <modelVersion>4.0.0</modelVersion>

 <groupId>org.roboguice</groupId>
 <artifactId>calculator</artifactId>
 <version>1.0-SNAPSHOT</version>
 <packaging>apk</packaging>
 <name>calculator</name>
```

As with every XML file, start with schemas and namespaces

groupId, artifactId, version, and packaging establish unique identifier for artifact in repository, and in general (like coordinates)

The final build will end up in $MVN_REPO/groupId/artifactId/version. The common example is to use the groupId as your project name and the artifactId as your module name. In this particular case, Manfred had used org.roboguice as groupId because it's an example for the roboguice project. The artifactId, calculator, identifies this example inside the project.

The last two attributes from this section are the packaging and the name. The packaging tells Maven the final output. Although the default is jar, Manfred had picked apk because he needs an Android application. The name in conjunction with the version will determine the output filename.

The second section to analyze is dependencies. Because the dependencies list is long, we'll analyze only a few of them. The dependencies section is the following:

```xml
<dependencies>
    <dependency>
      <groupId>org.roboguice</groupId>
      <artifactId>roboguice</artifactId>
      <version>2.0-SNAPSHOT</version>
    </dependency>

    ...

    <dependency>
      <groupId>com.google.android</groupId>
      <artifactId>android</artifactId>
      <version>2.3.3</version>
      <scope>provided</scope>
    </dependency>
```

1 Roboguice dependency

2 Android dependency

```
...
<dependency>
  <groupId>com.pivotallabs</groupId>                    ❸ Robolectric
  <artifactId>robolectric</artifactId>         ⟵┘          dependency
  <version>1.0</version>
  <scope>test</scope>
</dependency>
</dependencies>
```

Every dependency has four important attributes, `groupId`, `artifactId`, `version`, and `scope`. The first dependency is roboguice ❶. It has a `groupId`, `artifactId`, and `version`, which corresponds to a released version in some Maven repository. Remember what we learned in the first section? That information is required if someone needs to use your artifact as a dependency.

Although the roboguice dependency doesn't contain the `scope` attribute, you should know that `compile` is the default value. Compile dependencies are available in all classpaths of a project because they get included in the APK.

The next dependency is Android itself ❷. When you use Maven to build Android applications, you must always have Android as a dependency, but its `scope` is `provided`. `provided` is much like `compile`, but it indicates that you expect the JDK or a container to provide the dependency at runtime—in our case, the device running Android.

The last dependency is robolectric ❸. Robolectric is a test framework, so we only need that dependency when we're compiling/running the tests. That's what the `test` scope is for. This scope indicates that the dependency is not required for normal use of the application, and is only available for the test compilation and execution phases.

After the dependencies section in the pom.xml file, we have the `build` section, which has the `plugins` section inside. This is where you'll configure the Android Maven plugin. Let's take a look at the following code to see how it's done:

```
<build>
    <plugins>
      <plugin>
        <groupId>
          com.jayway.Maven.plugins.android.generation2
        </groupId>
        <artifactId>
          android-Maven-plugin                    ⟵┐ groupId, artifactId, and version
        </artifactId>                               ❶ for android-Maven-plugin
        <version>
          3.0.0-SNAPSHOT
        </version>
        <configuration>                           ⟵┐ android-Maven-
          <androidManifestFile>                    ❷ plugin configuration
            ${project.basedir}/AndroidManifest.xml
          </androidManifestFile>
          <assetsDirectory>
            ${project.basedir}/assets
          </assetsDirectory>
          <resourceDirectory>
```

```
      ${project.basedir}/res
    </resourceDirectory>

    <sdk>
      <platform>10</platform>
    </sdk>
    <undeployBeforeDeploy>
      true
    </undeployBeforeDeploy>
  </configuration>
  <extensions>true</extensions>
</plugin>

...

  </plugins>
</build>
```

Build plugins works in a way similar to dependencies. The previous code shows how the android-Maven-plugin gets configured ❶. If we were configuring a dependency, we'd need to provide a `groupId`, an `artifactId`, and a `version`.

You'll notice that Apache Maven follows the convention-over-configuration paradigm, which results in decreasing the number of decisions that developers need to make, gaining simplicity, but not necessarily losing flexibility. A great example of this approach can be seen where the android-Maven-plugin gets configured ❷. You might want to place the AndroidManifest.xml somewhere else so you have an attribute to modify the default location.

When the pom.xml is ready, you can treat your Android application as a Maven artifact. If you run the `mvn package`, you'll get a target directory with the APK inside. If you want to get the application installed in all attached devices, you can run `mvn android:deploy`.

48.1   The bottom line

Apache Maven is a great build tool. It's true that it's somewhat complicated the first time you use it, but after you understand how it works, you'll start to create a project by generating the pom.xml file.

The best way to learn about it is to read how someone else is using it. For example, you can examine the roboguice's pom.xml. You'll notice it's not hard at all.

48.2   External links

http://maven.apache.org/
https://github.com/mosabua/roboguice-calculator
http://code.google.com/p/maven-android-plugin/
https://github.com/roboguice/roboguice
www.robolectric.org
http://en.wikipedia.org/wiki/Convention_over_Configuration
www.simpligility.com

Hack 49 *Installing dependencies in a rooted device*
Android v1.6+

Android applications are commonly written in a dialect of Java and compiled to byte-code. Then they're converted from Java Virtual Machine–compatible .class files to Dalvik-compatible .dex files before installation on a device. Figure 49.1 (see section 49.5) illustrates the building process.

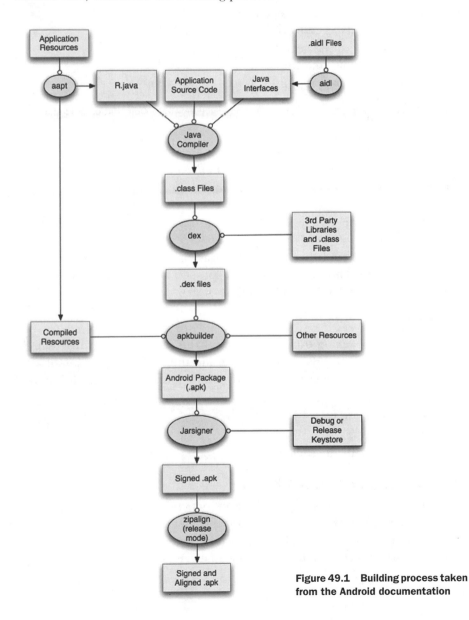

Figure 49.1   Building process taken from the Android documentation

Apart from the Android SDK, many third-party libraries are available that we can use as dependencies. These dependencies can be useful for improving your application functionality, code organization, customs views, and so on. As we add dependencies to our application, we might notice the build time increases. Android supports adding JAR dependencies, but it first needs to convert the JAR file's .class files to .dex every time we want to build, and this takes time. From our earlier figure, we narrow our focus to this sequence in figure 49.2.

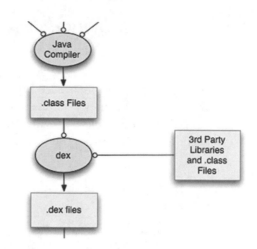

Figure 49.2 Compilation procedure

To give you an idea of how you can solve this, have you ever used Google's map library in Android? Remember how you added that dependency? The map library can be used from your application, but you never lose time indexing it. That's because the library is already installed on your device/emulator.

In this hack, we'll use the same approach, but with other libraries. We'll see how to install those dependencies in our developing device to make our build times faster, avoiding the dexing phase of the dependencies.

The first thing to understand from this hack is that we're installing dependencies on a rooted device. This means that this approach won't work for production. We're doing it to make our developing build times faster.

49.1 *Predexing*

The first step is predexing the dependencies. This means converting the JARs to dex. It can be done with the dx application inside the ANDROID_SDK/tools folder. For example, if our dependency is called dep.jar, we'll need to use the following line:

```
dx -JXmx1024M -JXms1024M -JXss4M
  --no-optimize --debug --dex
  --output=./dep_dex.jar dep.jar
```

The dep_dex.jar is the file that we'll upload to the device.

49.2 *Creating the permissions XML*

The second step is to create XML for each dependency with the permission to the library. If we think back to the Google maps dependency, when we want to use it we need to add a use-library tag in our AndroidManifest.xml file. The XML we'll create will be used for that specific line. Let's see an example:

```
<permissions>
  <library name="dep"          ◁————① Specifies library name
     file="/data/data/com.dep.package/files/dep_dex.jar"/>   ◁——┐  Writes path for
</permissions>                                                  ② predexed file
```

We first need to specify the library name ❶. This library name is the string that we should place in the use-library tag. We also need to write down the path for the pre-dexed file inside the device ❷. We can upload the predexed file using adb or using an Android application. An example of an application doing the installation is placed in the sample code. The application is a modification of Johannes Rudolph's scala-android-libs source code.

49.3 *Modifying AndroidManifest.xml*

The last step is to modify the AndroidManifest.xml file to use the dependencies installed in the device. The example for the dep mentioned previously would be like the following:

```
<uses-library name="dep"/>
```

That's it. We're now using dependencies from the device instead of compiling them every time we want to run the application. Remember to change the build tool to avoid compiling the dependencies. For instance, in Apache Maven we can set the scope to provided.

49.4 *The bottom line*

Installing dependencies is a great way to improve your application build time. I've been using it for some applications and I'm getting them built twice as fast.

Although this hack is useful, two things might bother you. First, you need a rooted device. Unfortunately, not all the Android devices are rootable. You'll also need to modify your build script to avoid this behavior when you're targeting production. Apache Maven would be a useful tool to handle different types of builds.

49.5 *External links*

http://developer.android.com/tools/building/index.html
https://github.com/scala-android-libs/scala-android-libs
http://android-argentina.blogspot.com/2011/11/roboinstaller-install-roboguice.html

Hack 50 *Using Jenkins to deal with device diversity*
Android v1.6+
Contributed by Christopher Orr

Testing Android applications can be tough. With hundreds of manufacturers producing thousands of unique Android models, a device is available to suit nearly every need. But for software developers, this ubiquity represents a challenge: how to ensure your application works well on all of these devices, and across a variety of screen sizes, hardware configurations, and Android OS versions.

Buying hundreds of devices to develop and test isn't feasible. Thankfully, Android provides a great resource system that enables you to support a diversity of devices and OS versions with a single application package. But verifying that you've used this system correctly requires a lot of testing: Did you mistype a view ID in your layout XML for layout-xhdpi-land? Are you missing a string parameter in one of the Japanese translations? With the bundled SQLite version often changing between Android releases, have you written a SQL query that works only on certain versions?

Testing your application on a few chosen devices—whether manually or using your automated test suite—is a possibility, but it's time-consuming and quickly becomes impractical as your application grows, adding more features plus support for further screen densities, device classes, and languages.

To reduce this burden, in this hack you'll automatically generate multiple Android emulators with various software and hardware properties and run your automated test suite on a number of them, allowing you to pinpoint potential problems on certain device configurations.

Although emulators can't fully replace testing on real hardware, they're a fast and flexible way to test how your application copes with a variety of hardware properties, such as whether the device has a front camera, is missing an SD card, has a hardware keyboard, is equipped with limited RAM, and so on.

You'll use a piece of software called Jenkins—a popular, open source continuous integration server, along with its Android Emulator plugin. The web-based dashboard of Jenkins can be seen in figure 50.1.

The strategy for this hack is to create a Jenkins "matrix" job and, for every check-in of your source code, you'll let Jenkins build your application, automatically generate some emulators, run your automated test suite on each of them, and then report on the results.

If you don't have an automated test suite already, you can create one relatively quickly using a library like Robotium—even starting with a few rudimentary smoke tests is helpful, such as ensuring that a few key activities open and that the expected UI elements are shown.

Assuming you have Jenkins running with the Android Emulator plugin installed, with a code repository containing both your application and test code that can be

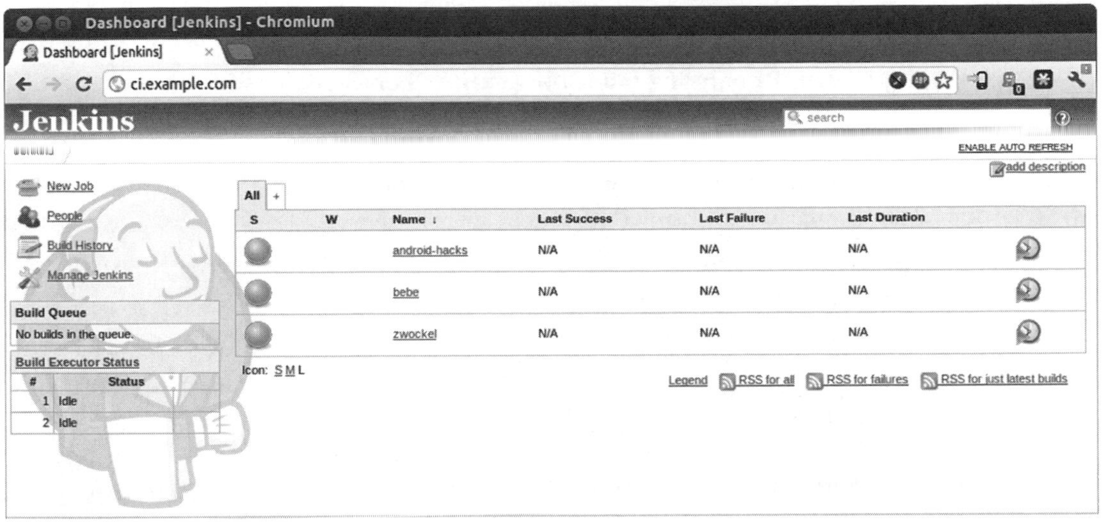

Figure 50.1   Jenkins dashboard UI

accessed by Jenkins (all of which is available in the sample code for this hack), the first thing to do is to choose the set of emulated devices you want to test with. As a minimum, you should test on each major Android OS version between your `minSdk-Version` and the latest version available. Other factors to think about are screen density, supported locales, and any hardware properties that are important to your application (e.g., camera, accelerometer).

50.1   Creating a Jenkins job

In Jenkins, click New Job, enter a job name, and select Build Multi-configuration Project" (also known as a "matrix" job) and click OK. Matrix jobs allow you to run the same set of steps—in your case, starting an Android emulator, building an application, and testing it—but with slight differences in configuration each time, such as changing the OS version used by the emulator.

In the job configuration, first enter the Source Code Management information to let Jenkins check out your application and test the code repository. Depending on the source control system you use, this may require you to install an extra plugin, such as the Git or Subversion plugin, via Jenkins' built-in plugin manager.

So that Jenkins monitors your repository for changes, enable the Build Periodically option and enter a cron-style syntax; for example, to poll for changes every two minutes on weekdays enter this:

```
*/2 * * * 1-5
```

Under the Configuration Matrix heading, click Add Axis, choose User-defined Axis, and in the Name field enter `os`. As the values, enter the following:

```
2.2 2.3.3 4.0.3 4.1
```

As you might be thinking, each value represents an Android version to test on. You could later add further axes for screen density, locales, and so on, but for now let's stick with just one. By entering four distinct values here, Jenkins will run four individual builds each time you start this job, with each build seeing a different value in the os environment variable.

Next, click Run an Android Emulator During Build, and enter the following values under Run Emulator with Properties:

- Android OS version: `${os}`
- Screen density: `240`
- Screen resolution: `WVGA`

You can leave the other fields unchanged, but you should uncheck the Show Emulator Window option. By setting the value `${os}` as the Android version, this ensures a different Android emulator will be created in each of the four builds that will occur. The complete configuration can be seen in figure 50.2.

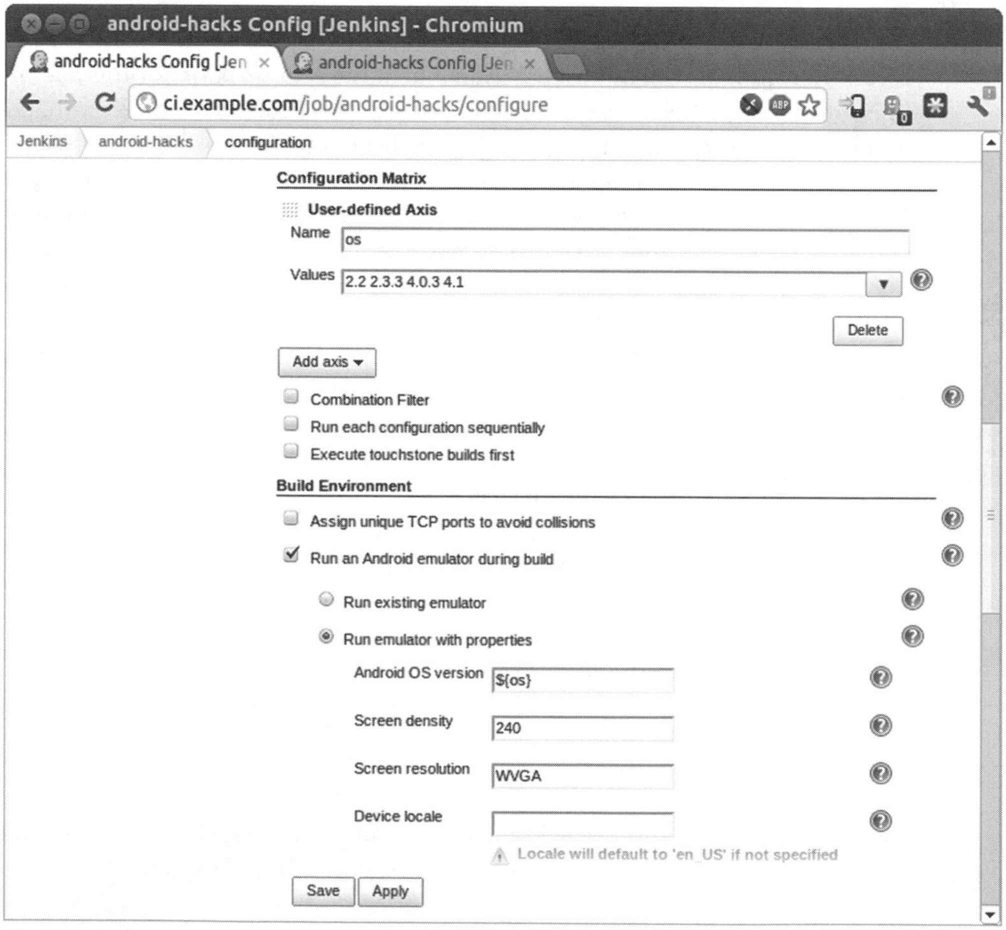

Figure 50.2   Configuring the axes and the emulator to create

Figure 50.3   Project page showing the configurations and a build in progress

In the Build section, add the build steps Install Android Project Prerequisites and Invoke Ant, assuming that you have used the android tool to generate Ant build scripts for your application and test projects. As the targets, enter `clean  debug  install test`. Click Advanced, and for the build file enter `tests/build.xml` (assuming `tests` is the directory name you've used for your test suite). Add a property: `sdk.dir=$ANDROID_HOME`.

If you have your Android test suite configured to output results in JUnit XML format (e.g., using the android-junit-report project), you can also check the Publish JUnit Test Result Report option under the Post-build Actions section.

Press Save to finalize the job configuration. You now have a Jenkins job that will run multiple times, each time checking out your source code, starting a different Android emulator, and then building your application and running its test suite. The job page should look like figure 50.3, with each ball representing one configuration (that is, OS version). They're gray to indicate that a build hasn't yet occurred.

50.2   *Running the job*

Click Build Now on the left side of the job page and, after a few seconds, you'll see a couple of the balls start to flash to indicate that a couple of the configurations are building.

Meanwhile, you can observe the build in progress by clicking on one of the flashing balls, and then clicking the blue progress bar on the left. This shows the Console Output, revealing that the source code has been checked out, an emulator has been automatically generated, and that Jenkins is waiting for the emulator to boot up.

By default, Jenkins runs two builds in parallel, so you'll have to wait a few minutes before everything completes. In any case, the first builds will take a little longer as the emulators have to be generated and booted for the first time. Furthermore, if you don't have the Android SDK installed on the machine where Jenkins is running, it will be automatically installed for you, which will add to the initial build time.

When the progress bars disappear from the Jenkins sidebar, the build is complete.

So within a few minutes you've automatically tested your software on four different versions of Android—and Jenkins will continue to do this automatically each time it finds a new commit in your code repository.

After you have the basics running, you can refine your Jenkins job configuration by adding further axes. For example, add an axis for different screen resolutions, allowing you to automatically create emulators to test layouts designed for different phone or tablet devices.

The Android Emulator plugin also lets you run the Android monkey tool to stress-test your UI. You could set up a Jenkins job that runs nightly, rather than for every commit, and that builds your APK, installs it onto an emulator, and then runs monkey against your application to check for instabilities.

50.3   *The bottom line*

Running your Android tests automatically means you can spend a lot less time manually testing your applications and lets you have greater confidence in the quality of your applications.

The samples for this hack include a basic Android application, test suite, and pre-configured Jenkins installation with which you can experiment.

Because Jenkins isn't only for automated testing, you can go beyond the basics of this hack and do things like integrating monkey testing into your workflow, check and monitor Android lint issues over time, automatically sign your APK, publish beta builds to a web server for testers, and much more.

50.4   *External links*

http://opensignalmaps.com/reports/fragmentation.php
http://jenkins-ci.org/
https://wiki.jenkins-ci.org/display/JENKINS/Android+Emulator+Plugin
https://wiki.jenkins-ci.org/display/JENKINS/Android+Lint+Plugin
https://github.com/jsankey/android-junit-report

index